The Senior's Guide to iPhone SE

The Step by Step Manual to Operate The Second Generation iPhone SE

Alec Young

Table of Contents

Introduction

The iPhone SE 2020 (a follow up to the 2016 iPhone SE) was launched in April 2020 as a new low-cost iPhone by the Apple brand. The phone comes with years of software updates, an amazing camera set and a topnotch performance even at its low cost. The Apple iPhone SE 2020 has several features in common with the much more expensive phones, like the A13 Bionic processor, which makes it as fast as the iPhone 11 series phones. The iPhone SE also has access to the 18W charging capability and the AI-enabled portrait mode that you will find in the iPhone 11, 11 Pro, and 11 Pro Max.

This user guide contains detailed steps on how to explore all the new features on your phone along with screenshots to make it easy for you to familiarize yourself with the workings of the operating system for iPhones. Whether you are just buying a new iPhone or downloading the new software to your existing device, this book would help you to achieve better and faster productivity.

iPhone SE 2020 Features

Design

While the latest addition to the Apple smartphones was named after the 2016 iPhone SE, the iPhone SE 2020 has similar features with the iPhone 8. The smartphone comes with a 4.7 inch display as well as thick bezels at the top and bottom. At the bottom of the phone, you have the Touch ID Home button and the top bezel has the speaker, front-facing camera and the accompanying sensors. At the back of the device you have the microphone, a single-lens rear camera, and an LED flash. The volume and mute switch buttons are located at the left side of the phone while the sleep/ wake buttons are at the right side. Just like the recent iPhone devices, the SE 2020 does not have a headphone jack, so you need to get Lightning or Bluetooth headphones.

Colors

The iPhone SE 2020 is available in three colors: space gray, red and white. All the colors have black front panels, the white version included.

Display

The 2020 iPhone SE has a 4.7 inch display plus a resolution of 1334 by 750. The phone features 625 nits maximum brightness, P3 wide display for strong vibrant colors, and multi-touch capabilities. The device offers the same Haptic Touch found on the iPhone 11 series. The Haptic Touch works the same way as the 3D Touch; however, it does not support various functions per press. It is also not pressure-sensitive.

Just like other iPhone and iPad models, the iPhone SE also supports True Tone. True Tone uses the ambient light sensor to discover lighting in a room, it then adjusts the intensity and temperature of the color to suit the light and give a more natural experience that is soft on the eyes.

Battery Life

The iPhone SE 2020 comes with a battery capacity of 1,821 mAh, same as the iPhone 8, which can last for up to 8 hours of streaming video playback, thirteen hours of video playback, and approx. forty hours of audio playback. The device also supports fast charging, meaning that the phone can be charged up to 50% in thirty minutes. However, the phone does not come with the USB-C power adapter for fast charging. You need to get that separately. The iPhone also supports Qi-based wireless charging as it is compatible with either the 7.5W or 5W Qi-based wireless charging accessory.

Camera

While the iPhone SE looks like the iPhone 8, its camera features adopted some technology from the latest iPhone series, thanks to the A13 Bionic Processor. The device's 12-megapixel camera has an f/1.8 aperture along with Smart HDR for enhanced shadow details and highlights, wide color capture, and optical image stabilization.

The phone does not support optimal zoom nor night mode as it does not have the multiple camera lenses that the iPhone 11 series have. Nonetheless, there is support for Depth Control, Portrait Lighting, and Portrait Mode, making it the first iPhone that enables Portrait Mode by making use of purely software solution.

You can also capture a **QuickTake** video with the front-facing camera of the iPhone SE 2020. It is the first iPhone with a front facing camera that supports this feature. The phone supports 1080p HD video recording at 30 frames per second (fps). Additional features for the front facing camera include the wide color capture, auto image stabilization, Retina Flash, auto HDR, and Burst Mode.

A13 Bionic

The phone has the A13 Bionic chip like the iPhone 11 series and this processor is known as the fastest chip ever amongst all smartphones. The processor is also more power-efficient, which causes less strain on battery life.

Touch ID

The iPhone SE 2020 features the home button with a Touch ID fingerprint sensor. Touch ID is used for confirming App Store purchases, confirming Apple Pay transactions, unlocking your iPhone, opening passcode-protected apps, and filling in passwords with iCloud Keychain.

Storage

The phone has three storage options: 256GB, 128 GB, and 64 GB along with a 3GB RAM.

Dust and Water Resistance

The iPhone SE 2020 has an IP67 water and dust resistance rating. This means that it can withstand up to 3.3 feet (one meter) of water for about thirty minutes. The device is also dust proof. However, it is important that you do not intentionally expose your device to water as Apple has warned users that the resistance is not permanent as the rating can reduce from normal wear and tear.

Chapter 1: Set Up Your iPhone SE

There are multiple options that you can use to set up your new iPhone. We will explore all the available options in this chapter.

Set Up Manually

Follow this option if you want to set up your new iPhone from scratch without importing data from an existing phone or device.

1. Press the power button until the Apple logo appears on your home screen. You will be welcomed with a "Hello" in multiple languages.
2. Tap your home button to begin.
3. Click on your preferred language from the displayed list.
4. Click on your **Country** or **Region.**

5. On the screen where you have the
   Quick Start option, click on **Set Up
   Manually.**

6. On the next screen, click on your Wi-Fi network or tap **Choose Another Network** to sign into a different Wi-fi address. If you would rather continue with a cellular connection, tap **Use Cellular Connection** (Make sure that your SIM card has already been inserted and that you are within your mobile network's service range).

7. Go through the **Data & Privacy** details from Apple, then click **Continue**.

8. You will receive a prompt to set up Touch ID. If you plan on setting up the Touch ID at another time, tap **Set Up Touch ID Later**. However, if you want to set it up now, click **Continue** and follow the prompts on your screen to capture your fingerprint

(thumb or finger) and set up your
Touch ID.

9. If you get a prompt to adjust your
grip, follow the directions to
continuously place the same finger
or thumb on the **Home button.** You
will be notified when your fingerprint
is fully captured as you will see a
"**Complete**" message. Click on
Continue at the bottom of the
screen.

10. The next screen is to create a 6-digit passcode for securing your data. You can also choose to go for a four digit passcode, no passcode or custom passcode. For this, click on **Passcode Options**.

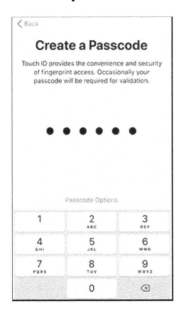

11. You will now get to the **App and Data** screen. Tap **Don't Transfer Apps and Data** to continue.

12. On the Apple ID page, enter your Apple ID and password or click on **Forgot password or don't have an Apple ID?** To create your own login details.

13. Go through the **Terms and Conditions**, then select **Agree**.

14. If prompted, in the screen for **Keep Your iPhone Up to Date**, select either **Install Updates Manually**, or **Continue**.

15. If prompted, select your choice for Location Services. To set up later, select **Skip Location Services**. To set it up now, select **Enable Location Services**.
16. If prompted, select your choice for Apple Pay. Choose either **Set Up Later in Wallet**, or tap **Continue** to set it up now.
17. Set up **Siri** or click on **Set Up Later in Settings** to do this at another time.
18. Set up **Screen Time** or click on **Set Up Later in Settings** to do this at another time.
19. Choose to share information with app developers or not.
20. Make your choice for True Tone Display. You can either choose to **See Without True Tone Display**, or click **Continue**. If you click on Continue, you will be taken to the **Appearance** screen, where you will get to explore

the **Light** or **Dark** options to know which you prefer. Tap **Continue.**

21. On the **Home Haptic Button** screen, try out the different numbers on the screen to see which you prefer, then tap **Continue.**

22. On the **Display Zoom** screen, select the best way you will like to use your home screen then tap **Continue.**

23. You will see the "Welcome to iPhone" screen. Click **Get Started** to begin exploring your new device.

Automatically Set Up Your iPhone

This option is for existing iPhone users who want to move their data and apps from their current phone to the new one.

1. Press the power button until the Apple logo appears on your home screen. You will be welcomed with a "Hello" in multiple languages.

2. Tap your home button to begin.
3. Click on your preferred language from the displayed List.
4. Click on your **Country** or **Region**.

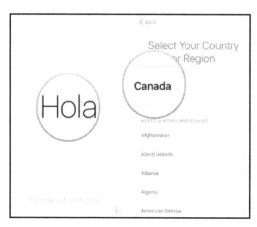

5. When you get to the next screen that displays the **Quick Start** option, place your new and previous devices beside each other and follow the prompt on your screen. You will see a bar-like image on your iPhone SE screen. Position the camera of your previous device over the image on your SE screen to sync your information from your previous iPhone to your iPhone SE.

6. Enter the passcode for your previous
   iPhone device.
7. After inputting the correct passcode,
   your screen will read "Setting up
   your iPhone".
8. The next step is to set up your Touch
   ID. If you plan on setting up the
   Touch ID at another time, tap Set Up
   Touch ID Later. However, if you want
   to set it up now, click Continue and
   follow the prompts on your screen to
   capture your fingerprint (thumb or
   finger) and set up your Touch ID.

9. If you get a prompt to adjust your grip, follow the directions to continuously place the same finger or thumb on the **Home button**. You will be notified when your fingerprint is fully captured as you will see a **"Complete"** message. Click on **Continue** at the bottom of the screen.

10.   The next screen is to create a 6-digit passcode for securing your data. You can also choose to go for a four digit passcode, no passcode or custom passcode. For this, click on Passcode Options.

Create a Passcode

Touch ID provides the convenience and security
of fingerprint access. Occasionally your
passcode will be required for validation.

● ● ● ● ● ●

Passcode Options

1	2 ABC	3 DEF
4 GHI	5 JKL	6 MNO
7 PQRS	8 TUV	9 WXYZ
	0	⊗

11. The next step provides you options to transfer data and apps to your new iPhone.

12. On the **Apps and Data** page, click on your preferred option and follow the prompts to move data and apps from your previous devices to your new iPhone SE. Click on **Don't Transfer Apps and Data** if you do not wish to move your data from your existing device.

Apps & Data

Choose how you want to transfer apps and data to this iPhone.

Restore from iCloud Backup

Restore from Mac or PC

Transfer Directly from iPhone

Move Data from Android

Don't Transfer Apps & Data

13. On the Apple ID page, enter your Apple ID and password or click on **Forgot password or don't have an Apple ID?** To create your own login details.

14. Go through the **Terms and Conditions**, then select **Agree.**

15. Your phone may send a prompt to move your settings from your old phone. This is shown in the Express Settings page. You can choose either to do so by tapping **Continue** or choose **Customize Settings**.

16. If prompted, in the screen for **Keep Your iPhone Up to Date**, select

either **Install Updates Manually**, or **Continue**.

17. If prompted, select your choice for Location Services. To set up later, select **Disable Location Services**. To set it up now, select **Enable Location Services**.

18. If prompted, select your choice for Apple Pay. Choose either **Set Up Later in Wallet**, or tap **Continue** to set it up now.

19. Set up **Siri** or click on **Set Up Later in Settings** to do this at another time.

20. Set up **Screen Time** or click on **Set Up Later in Settings** to do this at another time.

21. Choose to share information with app developers or not.

22. Make your choice for True Tone Display. You can either choose to **See Without True Tone Display**, or click **Continue**. If you click on Continue, you will be taken to the **Appearance**

screen, where you will get to explore
the **Light** or **Dark** options to know
which you prefer. Tap **Continue**.

23. On the **Home Haptic Button**
screen, try out the different numbers
on the screen to see which you
prefer, then tap **Continue**.

24. On the **Display Zoom** screen,
select the best way you will like to
use your home screen then tap
Continue.

25. You will see the "Welcome to iPhone" screen. Click **Get Started** to begin exploring your new device.

Transfer Data to iPhone SE from Your Mac

Move data from your Mac to your iPhone SE when setting up your phone for the first time.

1. The first step is to back up your old iPhone on the Mac. Plug the phone into your laptop.

2. Go to the Dock and click on the Finder icon.

3. Click on your iPhone under **Locations**.
4. Once prompted click on **Trust**.
5. Tick the box for **Encrypt Local Backup**.
6. You will need to set up a password if this is your first time to create an encrypted backup.
7. Tap **Back Up Now**.

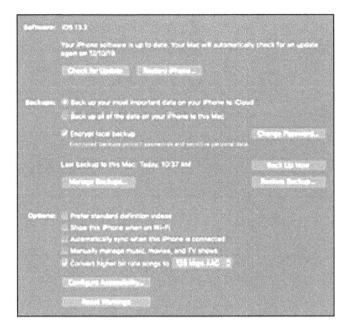

8. If you get a prompt to backup apps, you can skip it. This is because these apps will most likely be re-downloaded on the new device.

9. When you are done, disconnect your previous phone and power it off.

10.   Move the SIM from the previous iPhone to the new one if you desire.

11. Power on your new iPhone.

12. Press the home button to begin setting up your phone.

13. Click on your preferred language from the displayed List.

14. Click on your **Country or Region.**

15. On the screen where you have the Quick Set Up option, follow the steps described in the sections above to manually set up your phone or to use the **Quick Start** option till you get to the **Apps and Data** screen.

16. Plug your iPhone SE to your computer.

17. Tap **Restore from Mac or PC**

18. On your Mac, go to the Dock and click on the **Finder** icon. Under **Locations**, select **new iPhone**.

19. Then tap **Restore from this backup.**

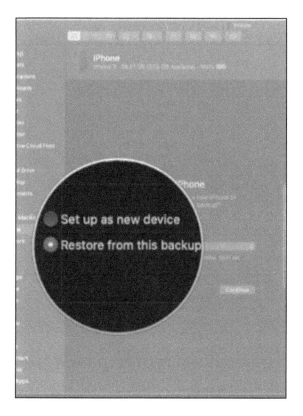

20.   Click on the most recent backup from the drop-down list. You will also see the date and size of each backup to help you tell the one you want to restore.

21. Tap **Continue.**

22. Type your encrypted password and click **Restore**.

23. When the restore process is complete, proceed with the remaining set up.

Transfer Data to your iPhone using iCloud

When setting up your iPhone, you may choose to move your data from iCloud with the steps below:

1. Open the settings app on your previous iPhone.
2. Click on your Apple ID link.
3. Tap **iCloud.**
4. Then tap **iCloud Backup** and click on **Back Up Now.**

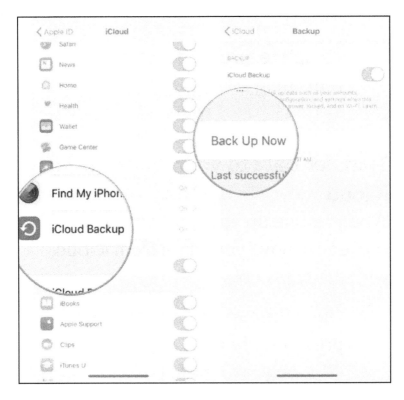

5. Once the backup is complete, power off the phone.
6. Move the SIM from the previous iPhone to the new one if you desire.
7. Power on your new iPhone.
8. Press the home button to begin setting up your phone.
9. Click on your preferred language from the displayed List.

10. Click on your **Country** or **Region.**
11. On the screen where you have the Quick Set Up option, follow the steps described in the sections above to manually set up your phone or to use the **Quick Start** option till you get to the **Apps and Data** screen.
12. Tap **Restore from iCloud backup.**
13. Log in to iCloud with your Apple ID and password.
14. Tap **Next.**
15. Agree to the **Terms and Conditions.**
16. **Agree** again
17. Find the most recent backup and click on it. The date and size will help you to locate the backup of your choice.
18. Wait for process to complete, then proceed with the remaining set up.

Transfer Data to Your iPhone Using "Move to iOS"

This option is for Android users who wish to move their data and apps from their Android devices to their iPhone. Again, you can only do this when setting up your iPhone for the first time.

1. Plug both phones into power.
2. Make sure that your iPhone SE has enough space to hold the contents you are moving.
3. Connect your Android device to an active Wi-fi.
4. Search for **Move to iOS** in your **Google Play Store.**
5. Click on the app, then tap **Install** to download it to your phone.
6. **Accept** permission request.

7. Power on your iPhone SE.

8. Press the home button to begin setting up your phone.

9. Click on your preferred language from the displayed list.

10.   Click on your **Country** or **Region.**

11. On the screen where you have the Quick Set Up option, follow the detailed steps mentioned in the sections above to manually set up

your phone or to use the **Quick Start** option till you get to the **Apps and Data** screen.

12. Select **Move Data from Android.**

13. Launch the "Move to iOS" app on your Android device, then tap **Continue** on the iPhone and Android.

14. Read the Terms and Conditions and tap **Agree.**

15. Go to your Android and click **Next.**

16. A code will come into your
iPhone, type the exact code on the
Move to iOS screen.

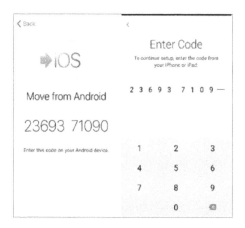

17. Your Android device will now
connect to your iPhone SE using the
Wi-fi connection.

18. Select the data that you want
to move, then click on **Next.**

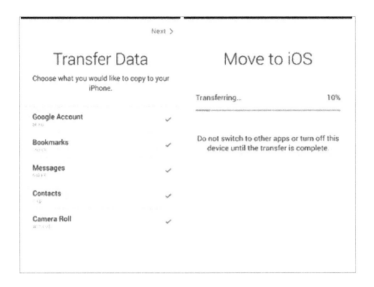

Transfer Data

Choose what you would like to copy to your
iPhone.

Google Account

Bookmarks

Messages

Contacts

Camera Roll

Move to iOS

Transferring...   10%

Do not switch to other apps or turn off this
device until the transfer is complete.

19.   Wait for the loading bar to read
100%, then tap **Done** on your
Android.

20.   Tap **Continue** on your iPhone to
continue setting up your phone.

Erase Your Device

If you have set up your device but wish to
restore data from your previous phone,
you will need to erase your iPhone and
start the setup process from scratch.
Follow the steps below to erase the
iPhone SE:

1. From the Settings app, tap **General.**
2. Click on **Reset.**
3. Then select **Erase All Content and Settings** to wipe off your iPhone and restart your device.

Chapter 2: Basic Settings

Power Off Your iPhone

To power off your iPhone,

1. Touch and hold down the power/
   side button until a slider appears on
   your screen.
2. Move the power off slider to the
   right to power off your screen.

Power On Your iPhone

1. Touch and hold down the power/
   side button until you see the Apple
   logo on your screen.

2. You will be prompted to input your passcode, if available.

3. Tap the home button to access the home screen.

Perform a Forced Reset

Forced resets are helpful for times when your device refuses to respond. It restarts the phone and clears whatever issue was hampering the phone's performance.

1. Quickly press and release the **Volume Up** button.
2. Quickly press and release the **Volume Down** button.

3. Touch and hold down the power/ side button until your phone restarts.

Haptic Touch

Pressing long on an item or app will cause a contextual menu to appear on your screen. This is what is known as Haptic Touch. In order to get familiar with this feature, press and hold on an icon, link, app, or menu, to view the options that show up. However, it is important to note that you will be unable to use this feature on lock screen notifications. The notification first have to be swiped left, after which you can click on 'View'.

Customize Haptic Touch

This option allows you to customize the speed at which the Haptic Touch should work, either Slow or Fast.

1. Launch the Settings app.
2. Tap **Accessibility.**

3. Click **Touch.**
4. Select **Haptic Touch.**
5. Then choose your preference in the displayed option: **Fast** or **Slow.**

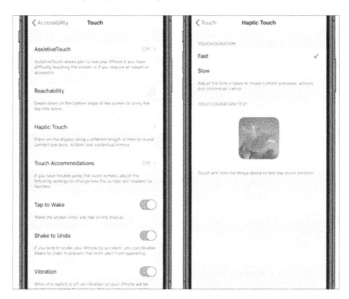

Set up Keyboard Shortcuts

With this feature on your iPhone, you can use characters to replace commonly used text. So, whenever you need to type a word, just insert the character and the word will pop up on your screen/ document.

1. Tap **General** in the **Settings** app.

2. Scroll down and select **Keyboard.**
3. Click on **Text Replacement.**

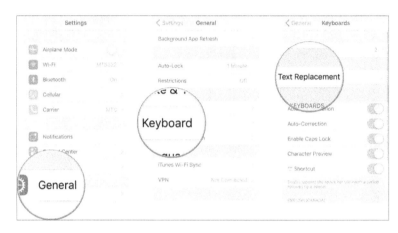

4. Tap ⊕.
5. In the Phrase field, type in the full phrase to link to a character.
6. In the Shortcut field, choose the character or snippet that you want to link to the full phrase.
7. Tap **Save** to store your changes.
8. When next you want to type this full phrase, just type the associated snippet or character and the full phrase will show on your keyboard.

Click your space bar or click on the phrase to select it.

Edit Keyboard Shortcuts

Follow the steps below to edit your keyboard shortcuts.

1. Tap **General** in the Settings app.
2. Tap **Keyboard.**
3. Click on **Text Replacement.**
4. Tap the shortcut that needs editing.
5. Make your changes.
6. Click **Save.**

Delete Keyboard Shortcuts

1. Tap **General** in the Settings app.
2. Tap **Keyboard.**
3. Click on **Text Replacement.**
4. Swipe left on the shortcut you want to delete.
5. Tap **Delete.**

Chapter 3: Apple ID

The Apple ID also authorizes you to make use of iMessages and Facetime within the Messages apps, Contacts via iCloud, Reminders, sync Calendars, buy books, movies, and music from iTunes, and also download and install games and apps.

Create an Apple ID

If you did not create your Apple ID when setting up your phone, follow the steps below to set it up now.

1. Launch the **Settings** app and click on **Sign into Your iPhone** at the top of your screen.

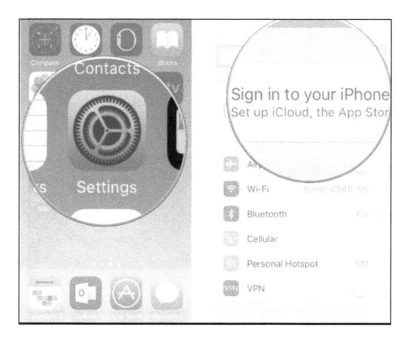

2. Select **Don't have an Apple ID or forgot it?**
3. Then click on **Create Apple ID.**

4. Type your birth date and click **Next**.

5. Type your names and click **Next**.

6. You may make use of your current email address to sign up, or register for a free iCloud email address.

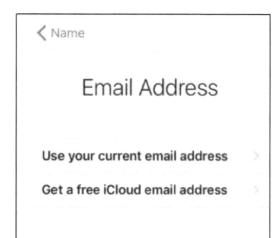

7. Type your email address and your new password.
8. Type the password again to reconfirm.
9. Select a security question and enter in the answer. Repeat until you have set three security questions and answers.
10.   Tap **Next.**

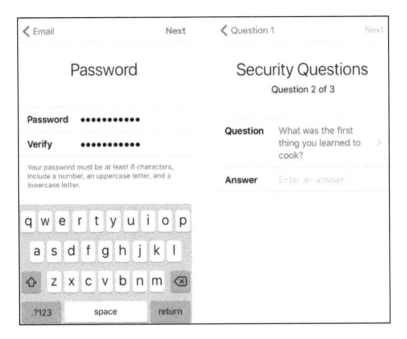

11. Read the Terms and Conditions and tap **Agree.**

12. Click on **Don't Merge** or **Merge** to sync data from your reminders, safari, contacts and calendars.

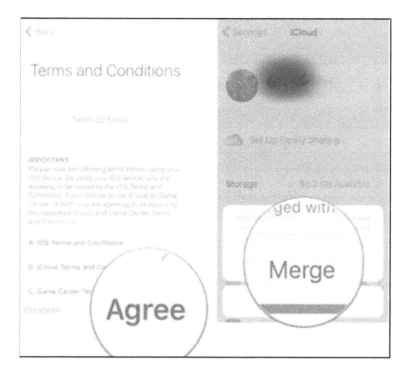

13. Tap **Ok** if you want to confirm that **Find My** has been enabled.

Sign In to iCloud with an Existing Apple ID

If you already created an Apple ID account, follow the steps below to sign into Apple ID on your new phone.

1. Launch the **Settings** app and click on **Sign into your iPhone**, this is located at the top of your screen.
2. Type your Apple ID and password. Tap **Sign In.**

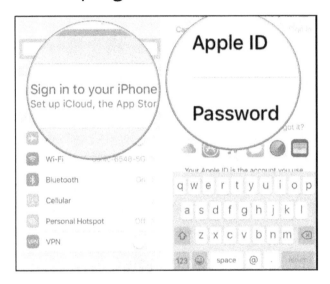

3. If you previously set up a passcode, you will need to type it in.
4. Ensure that you like the way your iCloud Photos are set up. Enable or disable iCloud photos.

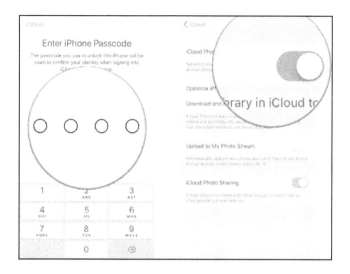

5. Check to confirm that **Apps using iCloud** is set up properly, by enabling or disabling them.

Sign Out of iCloud

1. Launch the **Settings** app and click on **your Apple ID** (this can be found at the top).
2. Scroll down to the end of your screen and tap **Sign Out.**

3. Type your Apple ID password. Tap **Turn Off.**

4. Make a selection of the data you would like to retain a copy of on your device, then enable that by toggling on the switch.

5. Tap **Sign Out** at the upper right part of the screen.

6. If prompted, tap **Sign Out** a second time to log out of iCloud.

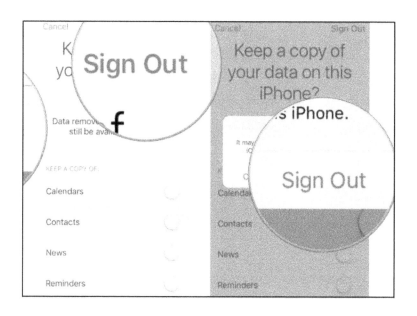

Chapter 4: Touch ID

Set Up Touch ID

Follow this step to set up your Touch ID if not done at the phone set up stage, or to include additional fingers.

1. Click on **Touch ID & Passcode** in the Settings app.
2. Enter in your passcode. If you haven't created this yet, you will need to create one to be able to set up Touch ID.
3. Select **Add a Fingerprint.**

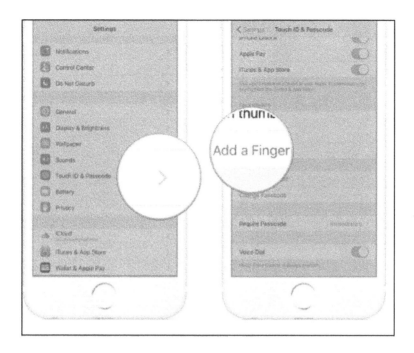

4. Place one finger on your home button until your phone vibrates. Continue to lift and place the finger whenever your phone vibrates, until you have filled the image on your screen.

5. Tap **Continue.**

6. Place the same finger on your home button until you have covered all the sides of the image on your screen.

7. Tap **Continue** and you will get a **Complete** notification on your screen.

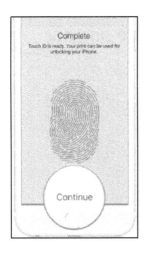

8. Tap **Continue** to conclude. Repeat step 1 to 8 until you have added up to five fingers, if desired.

Verify a Touch ID Fingerprint

If after registering multiple fingerprints, you are unsure of which fingerprint belongs to which finger, you can check and verify. This is important to know so as not to delete or rename the wrong fingerprints.

1. Click on **Touch ID & Passcode** in the **Settings** app.
2. Enter in your passcode.
3. Place your fingerprint (that has been registered) on the home button.
4. Try to find the label that changes color when you do this. It will change from white to gray.
5. Repeat this with all your registered fingerprint until you can tell which finger is used.

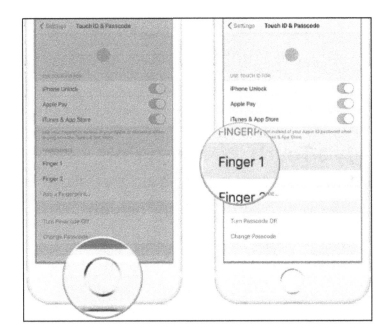

Tag or Provide Names for Your Touch ID Fingerprint

Giving a name to your fingerprints will help you to easily identify them. Follow the steps below to do this.

1. Click on **Touch ID & Passcode** in the **Settings** app.
2. Enter your passcode.

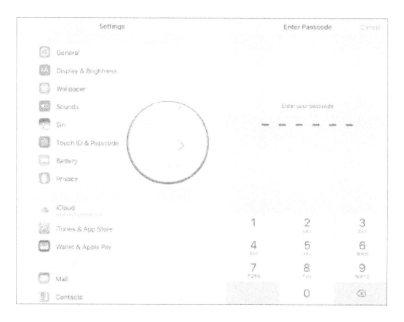

3. Tap the fingerprint you wish to rename.

4. Enter in the new name and click **Done.**

5. If you have more than one fingerprint saved, repeat the steps above for the remaining fingerprints.

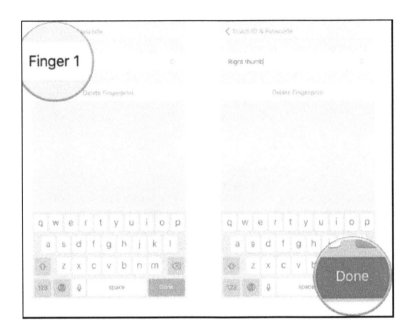

Disable Touch ID

If you prefer stronger security on iTunes, Apple Pay, app stores and lock screen, you can disable Touch ID and set up a strong alphanumeric password.

1. Click on **Touch ID & Passcode** in the **Settings** app.
2. Type your passcode.
3. Under **Use Touch ID For,** toggle off the switch for each option that you want to disable.

Delete a Fingerprint

Whenever you choose to delete a fingerprint, follow the steps below.

1. Click on **Touch ID & Passcode** in the **Settings** app.
2. Enter your passcode.
3. Select the fingerprint you wish to remove.
4. Tap **Delete Fingerprint.**

5. Scroll to the bottom of your screen and tap **Done.**
6. Another way to delete a fingerprint is to make a left swipe on the fingerprint you wish to remove

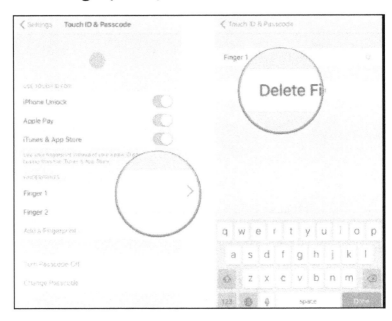

Unlock Your Phone with Touch ID

From the lock screen, place any of your registered fingers on the home button to unlock your phone.

Authorize Purchases Using Touch ID

If you wish to authorize your purchases on iTunes, Apple Books, and App store using Touch ID follow the steps below.

1. Click on **Touch ID & Passcode** in the Settings app.
2. Enter your passcode.
3. Switch on the options for iTunes and App Store.

4. Open the iTunes store, App store, or Apple Books.

5. Select the item you want to
   purchase; your phone will then
   prompt you for your Touch ID.

6. **Press on your home button (with the
   registered finger) to complete the
   purchase.**

Chapter 5: Apple Pay

Set up Apple Pay for easy online and in-store payment on your iPhone. With Apple Pay, it is more secure and easier to make credit card and debit card purchases.

Add a Card for Apple Pay

1. Open the Wallet app on your device.

2. Click the ⊕ button.

3. Click **Next.**

4. You may manually input your card details or scan your card if you have a debit or credit card with embossed numbers in front.
5. Tap **Next.**
6. Type your card's security code and expiry date.

7. Tap **Next.**

8. Read the Terms and Conditions and tap **Agree.**

9. Click **Agree** a second time.

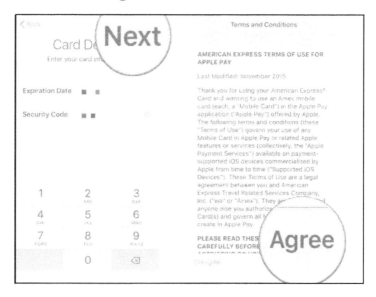

10.   Choose your preferred method for verification and tap **Next.**

11. Tap **Enter Code.**

12. Type in the code sent to you via your selected verification method.

13. Tap **Next,** then click **Done.**

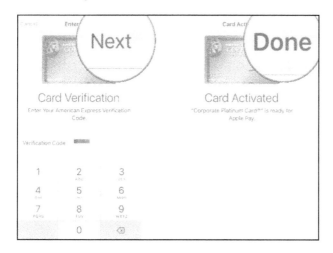

14.   In case you have more than one card you want to add, repeat the steps above to add the remaining cards.

Remove a Card from Apple Pay

1. Tap **Wallet and Apple Pay** in the **Settings** app.
2. Select the card that you would like to remove.
3. Tap **Remove Card** at the bottom of your screen to remove the card on your iPhone SE

Note that this change will only affect your iPhone SE. Follow the same step to remove the card on other linked devices.

Change the Default Card for Apple Pay

You can add several debit and credit cards to your Apple Pay account. However, it is always simpler and faster to have a default card in place for transactions. Set up a default card for a quick and easy payment process.

1. Tap **Wallet and Apple Pay** in the **Settings** app.
2. Click **Default Card.**

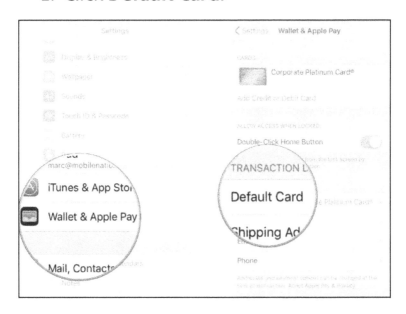

3. Select the card that you prefer to be your default card.
4. This way, on your next payment you may just proceed to complete the transaction using your default card.

Remotely Delete Your Card from Apple Pay

You can choose to delete Apple Pay from more than one device at the same time. This action will automatically delete all the linked cards on Apple Pay.

1. Go to www.iCloud.com on your browser.
2. Log in using your Apple ID details.
3. Tap **Settings.**

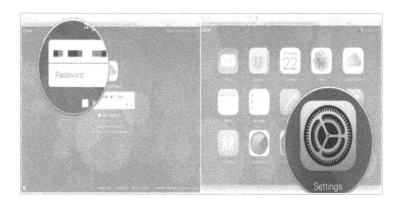

4. Click on the desired devices under
   My Devices. The Apple logo will
   appear beside the devices that have
   an Apple Pay account.

5. Tap **Remove All** to delete Apple Pay
   from all the selected devices.

Chapter 6: Hey Siri

When setting up your new phone for the first time, you get the option to set up Siri (Apple's virtual assistant) at that time. However, this guide will help you set up Siri if you are yet to do so.

Turn on "Hey Siri"

1. Tap **Siri and Search** from within the **Settings** app.
2. Move the switch beside **Listen for "Hey Siri"** to the right to enable it.

3. Tap **Enable Siri** on the next screen.

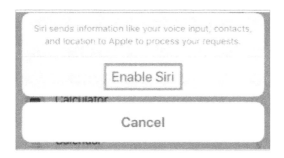

Train Siri to Recognize Your Voice

After you complete setting up Siri, you will need to train it to recognize your voice.

1. After enabling Siri, tap **Continue.**

2. Make use of your voice to say, **"Hey Siri"**.
3. Then repeat the words on your screen to help the virtual assistant recognize your voice.
4. Each time you read back to Siri what is on your screen, you get the check mark.

5. Tap **Done** to start using Siri.

"Hey Siri" Is Ready

Siri will recognize your voice whenever you say, "Hey Siri."

Done

Use "Hey Siri"

Below are tips on how to use Siri seamlessly:

1. Stay close to your phone.
2. Say "Hey Siri" clearly, so your phone is be able to pick it up.
3. Followed by what you want Siri to do. For example, say "Hey Siri", followed by, "What time is it in Dubai?".

Activate Siri From Home Button

Follow the steps below to activate Siri when pressing and holding down your Home button:

1. Tap **Siri and Search** from within the **Settings** app.
2. Move the switch beside **Hey Siri** and **Press Home for Siri** to the right to enable the two options.

3. Tap **Enable Siri** on the next screen to complete the set up.

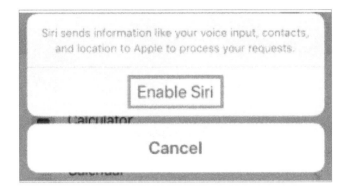

Change Siri's Language

Follow the steps below to choose your preferred language for communicating with Siri:

1. Tap **Siri and Search** from within the **Settings** app.

2. Click on **Language** and choose your preferred language.

Access Siri on Lock Screen

Enable this option if you want to be able to use Siri even on your lock screen.

1. Tap **Siri and Search** from within the **Settings** app.
2. Move the switch beside **Allow Siri When Locked** to the right to enable it.

Change Siri Voice

Set up Siri to speak to you in your preferred accent.

1. Tap **Siri and Search** from within the **Settings** app.
2. Tap **Siri Voice** and choose your preference.

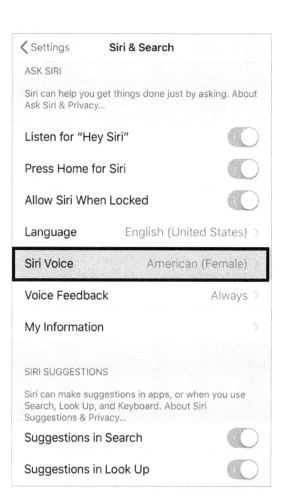

Chapter 7: Contacts

We will explore how to add contacts as well as use the Contacts app on the iPhone SE.

Add a Contact

Follow the steps below to add a contact:

1. Tap the **Contacts** app to open it.

2. Tap ⊕ at the top right side of your phone.
3. Enter the name and other details of the contact.

4. Click ⊕ to enter the phone number of the contact.

5. Usually, **Home** will be the default option used for the contact's number. If you want to change this, select the arrow beside **Home** to explore other options (for example, mobile, work, and so on).

6. Click on **Done** to complete saving that contact.

Delete a Contact

1. Open the **Contacts** app.
2. Select the contact you would like to delete.
3. Select **Edit** on the top-right area of your screen.
4. Then scroll down towards the end of the screen and tap **Delete Contact**. Note that this does not stop the person from contacting you, if that's what you want, you would have to block them.

Update Existing Contact

You can make changes to already existing contact. Here's how:

1. Open the **Contacts** app.
2. Select the contact you would like to update.
3. Select **Edit** on the top-right area of your screen.
4. Change the information that needs updating.
5. Click on **Done.**

Find an Existing Contact

There are a couple ways to find a contact in your phone:

Method 1

This is a fast way to search for a contact.

1. Open the **Contacts** app.
2. Tap the search bar (this is at the top of the page).

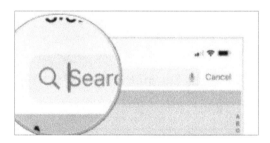

3. Begin to type the name of your contact. The suggestion list will continue to modify as you type.
4. Click on the contact once it is displayed on the search result.

Method 2

This method is for times when you are unable to remember the full names of the contact but can remember the first few letters in the name. A browse in connections is one sure way of finding that contact.

1. Open the **Contacts** app.
2. On the right corner of the page, click on the preferred letter. Depending on your settings, after you have clicked on a letter, you will immediately see contacts whose last name or first name begins with that letter.

3. Now scroll through the contacts until you find the individual whose contact you are looking for.

Assign Photos to Contacts

You can also assign pictures to contacts with the steps below:

1. Launch the **Photos** app.
2. Open the photo you want to use for a contact.
3. Tap  at the bottom left.
4. Then tap **Assign to Contact.**

5. Select the contact.

6. Drag the picture until you get the look that you want.
7. Scroll to the bottom of your screen and click **Choose.**
8. Then tap **Update** to finish.

Share a Contact

Follow the steps below to share your contact directly from the Contacts app:

1. Tap the contact you want to share on the **Contacts** app.
2. On the next screen, tap **Share Contact.**

3. On the Share sheet, choose the method you want to use to send the contact.
4. Send.

Block Contacts in the Phone App

Follow the steps below to prevent a contact from contacting you in the future:

1. Open the **Phone** app.
2. Scroll down and tap either the **Recents** or **Contacts** button.
3. If in the Recents tab, tap ⓘ by the side of the contact you want to block. If in the Contacts tab, click on the contact to open it.
4. Tap **Block This Contact.**
5. Tap **Block Contact** to complete your action.

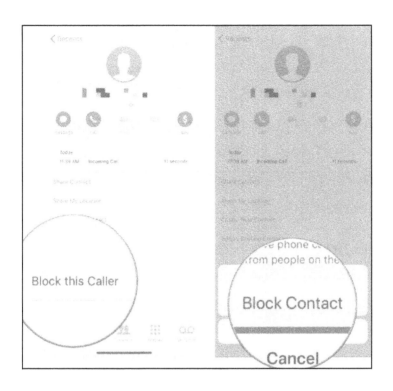

Block this Caller

Block Contact

Cancel

Chapter 8: Using Screen Time

A lot of us spend more time on our phones than we should. Screen Time on iPhone SE gives you a graphical picture of the time spent on your phones. The feature also allows you to set a limit on the time spent on specified apps and websites.

Enable Screen Time

Follow the steps below to enable Screen Time:

1. Launch the **Settings** app.
2. Tap **Screen Time.**
3. Select **Turn On Screen Time.**

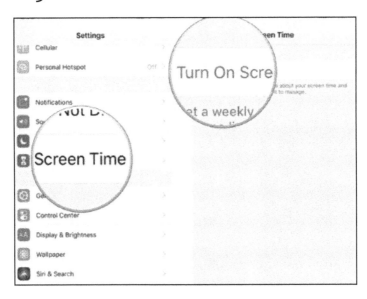

4. Tap **Continue** to proceed.
5. Select **This is My iPhone.**

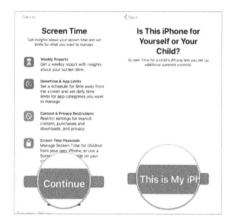

Disable Screen Time

Here is how to disable screen time on your device:

1. Launch the **Settings** app.
2. Tap **Screen Time.**
3. Select **Turn Off Screen Time.**

Create Downtime

Downtime allows you to schedule a time that you are away from the screen. You have the option to allow some apps to be utilized during Downtime. Note that even with downtime activated, you will still be able to receive phone calls.

1. Launch the **Settings** app.
2. Tap **Screen Time.**
3. Select **Downtime.**

4. On the next screen, move the switch beside **Downtime** to the right to enable it.

5. Select a schedule for the downtime from the available options: **Customize Days** or **Every Day.**

6. If you choose **Customize Days,** set up the days that the downtime should happen.

7. Then choose the exact time of downtime for the selected days.

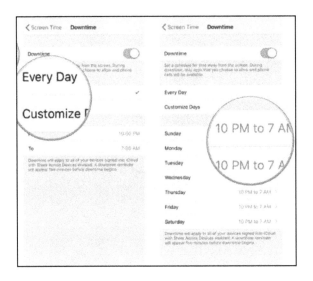

Set Up Always Allowed Apps

Each time you activate Downtime on your iPhone, you will be unable to access apps on your phone. However, you can choose to allow some specific apps to always be accessible irrespective of any limits that have been set up. Follow the steps below to do this:

1. Launch the **Settings** app.
2. Click on **Screen Time.**
3. Tap **Always Allowed.**

4. Tap the Plus  sign beside the apps you want to make always available. Click on the minus ⊖ sign for the apps that shouldn't fall into this category.

Activate Communication Limit

Screen Time also allows you to limit your communication with people through all available messaging apps. With this feature enabled, you will only be able to communicate with the selected contacts at specified time/duration.

1. Launch the **Settings** app.
2. Tap **Screen Time.**
3. Select **Communication Limits.**
4. Click on **During Allowed Screen Time** and select your preferred option, either **Contacts Only** or **Everyone.** You can also enable **Allow Introductions in Groups** (this option makes it possible to add others to group conversations only when a family member or one of your contacts is already in the group).
5. Click on **During Downtime** and select your preferred option, either **Specific Contacts** or **Everyone.**
6. If your choice is **Specific Contacts,** select **Add Contacts.**
7. Click on the method you want to use in getting the contacts: **Choose from my contacts, Add New Contact,** or **Choose from X Contacts.**

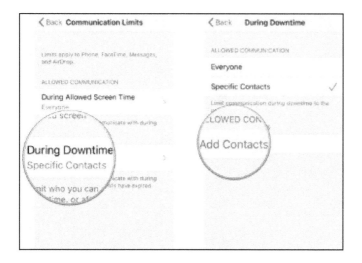

Combine Screen Time on All Apple Devices

To combine screen time on all your Apple devices that are logged in to the same iCloud account, follow the steps below:

1. Launch the **Settings** app.
2. Tap **Screen Time.**
3. Go to **Share Across Devices,** and move the switch to the right to enable the option and begin to view a combined screen time report across all your Apple devices.

Set Up App Limits

You can restrict the time you spend on specified apps, to give you time to do other important things. Once the set time is up, your phone will automatically block your access to the app for the rest of the day.

1. Launch the **Settings** app.
2. Tap **Screen Time.**
3. Select **App Limits.**

4. Then click on **Add Limit**.
5. Select all the app categories that you will like to place a limit on.

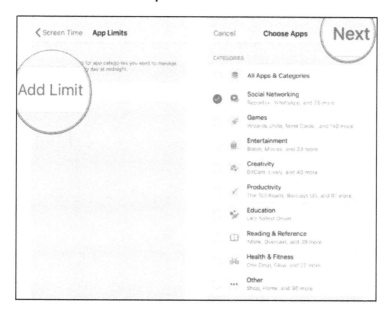

6. If you will rather limit certain apps within a category, click on the arrow by the right side of the category to display all the apps, then select the app that you want to limit.

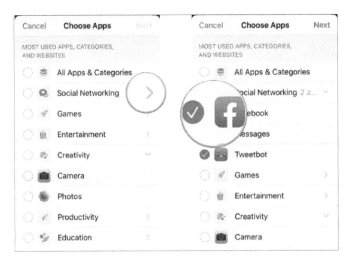

7. Tap **Next.**
8. Then allot time for all the apps that you selected.
9. Select the **Days** that the rules should work.
10.   Then click on **Add** to save your changes.

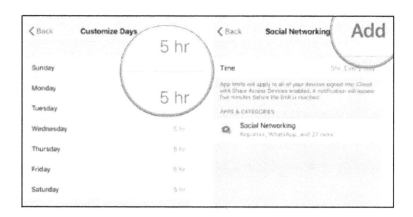

Customize Days	
Sunday	
Monday	
Tuesday	
Wednesday	5 hr
Thursday	5 hr
Friday	5 hr
Saturday	5 hr

< Back   Social Networking   **Add**

Time   5hr, Everyday

App limits will apply to all of your devices signed into iCloud with Share Across Devices enabled. A notification will appear five minutes before the limit is reached.

APPS & CATEGORIES

⚙ Social Networking
    Regram+, WhatsApp, and 27 more

Chapter 9: Activating Parental Control

For parents who may want to restrict the kind of contents their child can access on their phones, the parental control feature on the iPhone SE provides that privilege.

Turn on Restrictions

1. Launch the **Settings** app.
2. Tap **Screen Time.**
3. Select **Turn On Screen Time.**

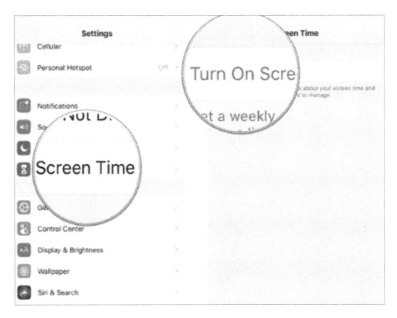

4. Select **Content & Privacy Restrictions.**
5. Type a four digit passcode.
6. Re-type the passcode.

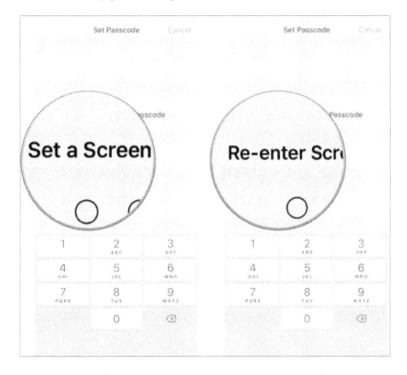

7. You have now set up parental passcode on your child's iPhone.

Set Up Content and Privacy Restrictions

Here is how to prevent your child from accessing or viewing inappropriate content on their device:

1. Launch the **Settings** app.
2. Tap **Screen Time.**
3. Click on **Content & Privacy Restrictions.**
4. Go to **Content & Privacy Restrictions** and move the switch to the right to enable the feature.
5. Click on each of the option that you want to modify.

6. For each option you click on, select either **Allow Changes** or **Don't Allow Changes.**

7. Go down to the section with the toggle and switch on or off any of the settings that you desire.

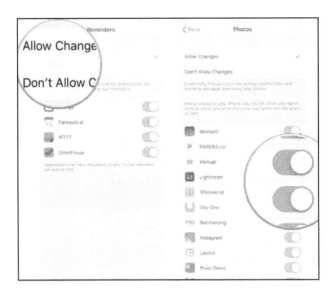

Block New Apps from Having Access to Phone Data

New apps always request for access to your phone's data. Here is how to restrict these apps from accessing your data:

1. Launch the **Settings** app.
2. Click on **Screen Time.**
3. Select **Content & Privacy Restrictions.**
4. Then select the data type that you do not want to share from the available options: **Share My Location, Reminders, Calendars, Location**

Services, Contacts, Photos, Media &Apple Music, Bluetooth Sharing, Microphone, and **Speech Recognition.**

5. For each data type you select, click on **Don't Allow Changes.** You can always come back to this step to **Allow Changes.**

Deny Access to Data From Specified Apps

Here is how to stop some apps from accessing your data:

1. Launch the **Settings** app.

2. Click on **Screen Time.**

3. Select **Content & Privacy Restrictions.**

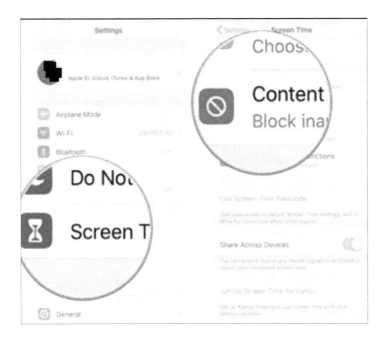

4. Then select the data type that you do not want to share from the available options.

5. Now click on the exact app you wish to restrict access for.

6. On the next screen, click on the kind of access that you want to assign to that app.

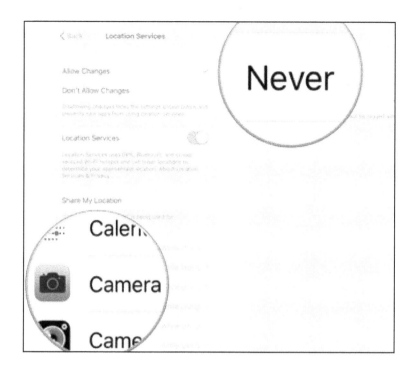

Restrict iBook Store Access

1. Launch the **Settings** app.

2. Click on **Screen Time.**

3. Select **Content & Privacy Restrictions.**

4. You will receive a prompt to enter your four digit passcode. Re-enter the code when prompted.

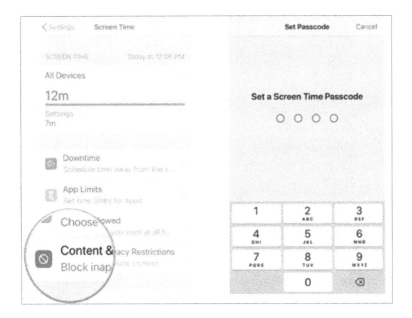

 Settings   Screen Time

SCREEN TIME   Today at 12:06 PM

All Devices

12m

Settings
7m

Downtime
Schedule time away from the s...

App Limits
Set time limits for apps

Choose owed

Content & acy Restrictions
Block inap iate content

Set Passcode   Cancel

Set a Screen Time Passcode

○ ○ ○ ○

1	2 ABC	3 DEF
4 GHI	5 JKL	6 MNO
7 PQRS	8 TUV	9 WXYZ
	0	⊗

5. Move to **Content & Privacy** and move the switch to the right to enable it, if it is not already enabled.

6. Click on **Allowed apps.**

7. Move the switch beside **Book Store** to the right to enable it.

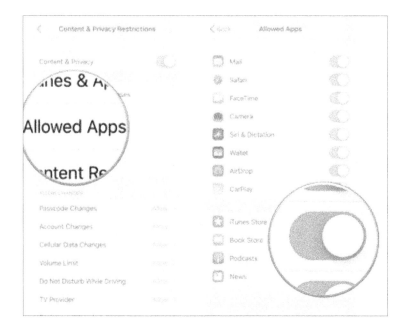

Restrict iTunes Store Access

1. Launch the **Settings** app.

2. Click on **Screen Time.**

3. Select **Content & Privacy Restrictions.**

4. You will receive a prompt to enter your four digit passcode. Re-enter the code when prompted.

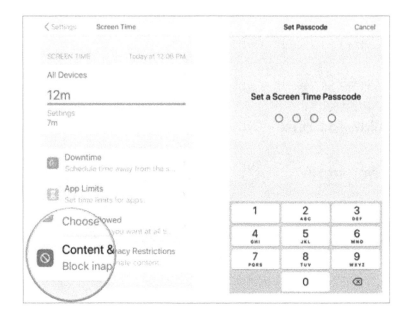

5. Move to **Content & Privacy** and move the switch to the right to enable it, if it is not already enabled.

6. Click on **Allowed apps.**

7. Move the switch beside **iTunes Store** to the right to enable it.

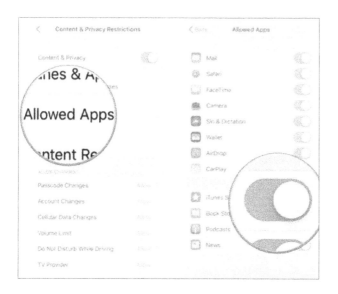

Block Access to Install Apps

1. Launch the **Settings** app.

2. Click on **Screen Time.**

3. Select **Content & Privacy Restrictions.**

4. You will receive a prompt to enter your four digit passcode. Re-enter the code when prompted.

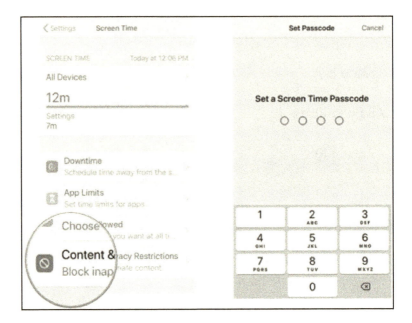

5. Move to **Content & Privacy** and move the switch to the right to enable it, if it is not already enabled.

6. Click on **iTunes & App Store Purchases.**

7. Select **Installing Apps.**
8. Click on **Don't Allow.**

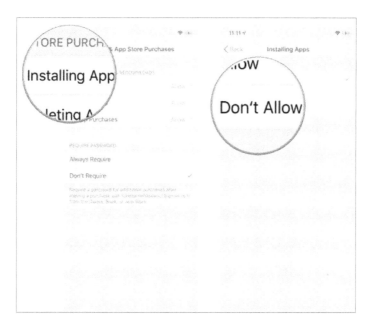

Block In-App Purchases

1. Launch the **Settings** app.
2. Click on **Screen Time.**
3. Select **Content & Privacy Restrictions.**
4. You will receive a prompt to enter your four digit passcode. Re-enter the code when prompted.

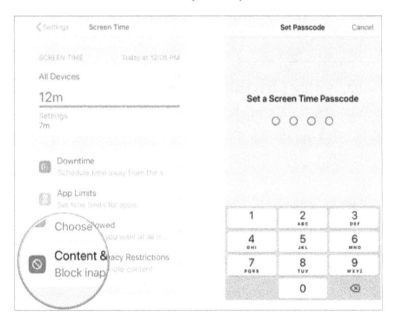

5. Move to **Content & Privacy** and move the switch to the right to enable it, if it is not already enabled.

6. Select **iTunes & App Store Purchases.**

7. Select **In-app Purchases.**
8. Then select **Don't Allow.**

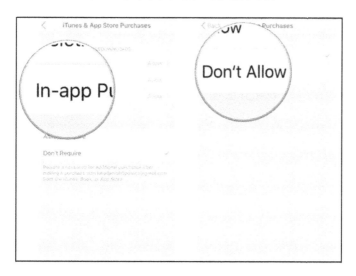

Always Require Password to Make Purchases

Set up your child's iPhone to always request for a password for any purchase made in the iTunes store, Book store and the App Store.

1. Launch the **Settings** app.
2. Select **Screen Time.**
3. Select **Content & Privacy Restrictions.**
4. You will receive a prompt to enter your four digit passcode. Re-enter the code when prompted.
5. Move to **Content & Privacy** and move the switch to the right to enable it, if it is not already enabled.
6. Select **iTunes & App Store Purchases.**
7. Select **Always Require.**

Screen Time for Your Kid

Follow the steps below to set up screen time for your kids:

1. Launch the **Settings** app.
2. Tap **Screen Time.**
3. Tap **Continue.**
4. Click on **This is My Child's iPhone.**
5. On the next screen, you will receive a prompt to set up Downtime for the child. Downtime is the specific time

in a day the child should not use the iPhone.

6. Tap **Start.**
7. Select the start time for the Downtime, then click on **Start** again.
8. Select the end time for the Downtime.
9. Select **Set Downtime** to complete the setting.

Set App Limit for Your Child

After successfully setting up screen time for your child, use this step to set up app limit on the child's iPhone SE.

1. After the **Set Downtime** screen, the next screen will be to set **App Limit.**

2. You will see different categories on your screen like Education, Health & Fitness, etc. Click on the desired category, go to the field for **Time Amount** and type in the desired time that your child can access the selected app each day.

3. Now click on **Set App Limit.** Follow these steps until you have set the limit for each of the desired app categories.

4. Read the Content and Privacy controls, then tap **Continue.**

5. Create a four digit passcode.

6. Re-type the passcode to complete setting up screen time on your child's iPhone.

Parent Passcode

Create a passcode that will be required to
allow for more time, or to make changes to
Screen Time settings.

○ ○ ○ ○

1	2 ABC	3 DEF
4 GHI	5 JKL	6 MNO
7 PQRS	8 TUV	9 WXYZ
	0	⌫

Parent Passcode

Re-enter your passcode

○ ○ ○ ○

1	2 ABC	3 DEF
4 GHI	5 JKL	6 MNO
7 PQRS	8 TUV	9 WXYZ
	0	⌫

Set Up Screen Time Passcode

1. Launch the **Settings** app.
2. Tap **Screen Time.**
3. Click on **Use Screen Time Passcode.**
4. Create a 4-digit passcode.
5. Re-type the passcode to complete the set up.

Disable Screen Time Passcode

1. Launch the **Settings** app.
2. Tap **Screen Time.**
3. Select **Change Screen Time Passcode.**

4. Select **Turn Off Screen Time Passcode** to disable passcode.

5. Type in your current passcode when prompted.

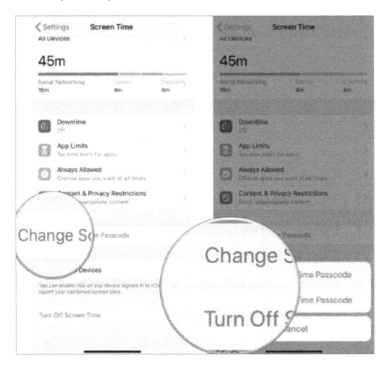

Modify Screen Time Passcode

1. Launch the **Settings** app.

2. Tap **Screen Time.**

3. Select **Change Screen Time Passcode.**

4. Then select **Change Screen Time Passcode** again to change passcode.

5. Type in your current passcode when prompted.

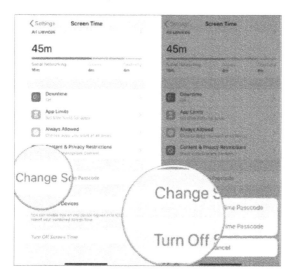

Prevent Deletion of Apps

1. Launch the **Settings** app.

2. Click on **Screen Time.**

3. Select **Content & Privacy Restrictions.**

4. You will receive a prompt to enter your four digit passcode. Re-enter the code when prompted.

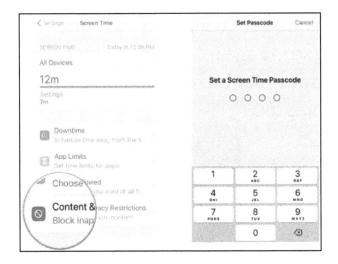

5. Move to **Content & Privacy** and move the switch to the right to enable it, if it is not already enabled.

6. Select **iTunes & App Store Purchases.**

7. Select **Deleting Apps.**
8. Select **Don't Allow.**

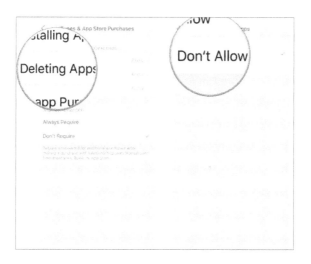

Block Adult Content in Safari

1. Launch the **Settings** app.
2. Select **Screen Time.**
3. Select **Content & Privacy Restrictions.**
4. Select **Content Restrictions.**
5. Then click on **Web Content.**
6. On the next screen, select **Limit Adult Websites.**

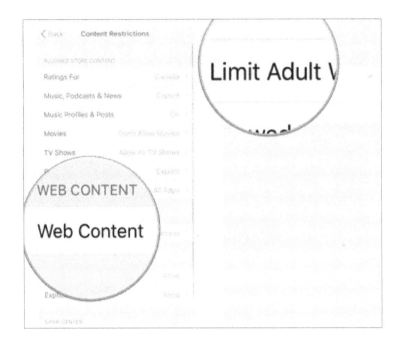

Block Specific Websites in Safari

There have been instances where some URL escaped the blocked list. All you need to do is copy the URL of the site, then follow the steps below to block that site.

1. Launch the **Settings** app.
2. Click on **Screen Time.**
3. Select **Content & Privacy Restrictions.**
4. Select **Content Restrictions.**

5. Then click on **Web Content.**

6. On the next screen, select **Limit Adult Websites.**

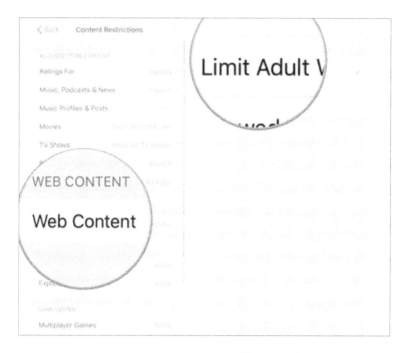

7. Navigate to **Never Allow,** then select **Add a Website.**

8. Input your desired website address on the next screen.

9. Tap **Done.**

10.   Follow this step to block all the sites that may have escaped the group blocking. You may also need

to block the mobile address for those
sites.

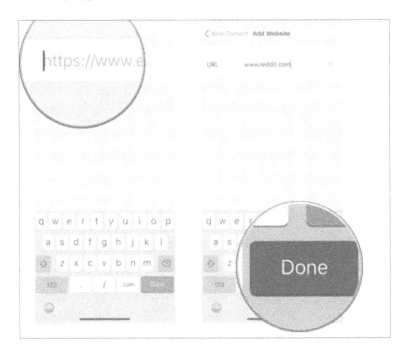

Block All Web Addresses Except For Whitelisted Sites in Safari

Follow the steps below to whitelist some sites like Apple:

1. Launch the **Settings** app.
2. Select **Screen Time.**

3. Select **Content & Privacy Restrictions.**
4. Select **Content Restrictions.**
5. Then click on **Web Content.**
6. Select **Allowed Websites Only.**

7. Select **Add Website.**
8. Input the desired website, then tap **Done** at the bottom of the screen.
9. Follow this step to whitelist all the desired websites, including their mobile versions.

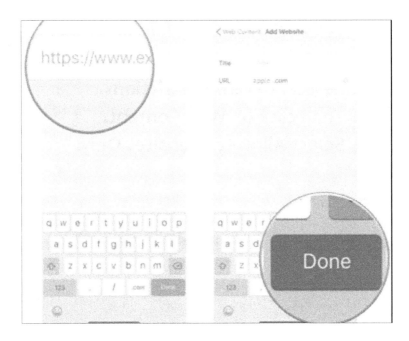

Restrict Music, Movies and TV Shows Based on a Region's Content Rating

1. Launch the **Settings** app.
2. Click on **Screen Time.**
3. Select **Content & Privacy Restrictions.**
4. Select **Content Restrictions.**
5. Select **Ratings For.**
6. Choose your desired region or country name to complete the setup.

Hide TV Shows in the Cloud

1. Launch the **Settings** app.
2. Select **Screen Time.**
3. Select **Content & Privacy Restrictions.**
4. Select **Content Restrictions.**
5. Select **TV Shows.**
6. Move the switch beside '**Show TV Shows in the Cloud**' to the right to enable. Move the switch to the left to turn off or disable.

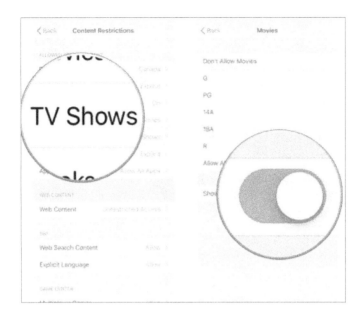

Hide Movies in the Cloud

To hide movies:

1. Launch the **Settings** app.
2. Select **Screen Time.**
3. Select **Content & Privacy Restrictions.**
4. Select **Content Restrictions.**
5. Select **Movies.**
6. Move the switch beside '**Show Movies in the Cloud**' to the right to

enable. Move the switch to the left
to turn off or disable.

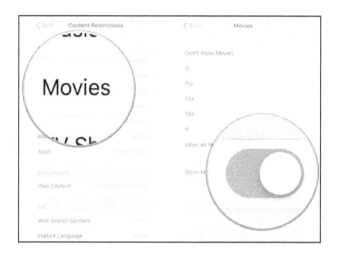

Block Explicit Content Using Ratings
Here is how to block contents that fall
within ratings of your choice:

1. Launch the **Settings** app.
2. Select **Screen Time.**
3. Select **Content & Privacy Restrictions.**
4. Select **Content Restrictions.**
5. Navigate to **Allowed Content** section, then tap each of the content types:

- Apps.
- TV shows.
- Movies.
- Music.
- Podcasts & News.

6. Select the highest rating that should be allowed on your phone.

Block Sexually Explicit Materials from iBooks

1. Launch the **Settings** app.
2. Select **Screen Time.**

3. Select **Content & Privacy Restrictions.**
4. Select **Content Restrictions.**
5. Select **Books.**
6. Then click on **Clean.**

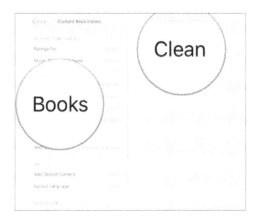

Stop Siri from Using Explicit Words

1. Launch the **Settings** app.
2. Select **Screen Time.**
3. Select **Content & Privacy Restrictions.**
4. Select **Content Restrictions.**
5. Scroll down to the Siri section and tap **Explicit Language.**
6. Select **Don't Allow.**

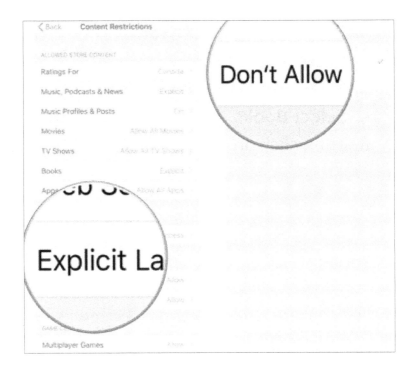

Restrict Access to Games Based on Ratings

1. Launch the **Settings** app.
2. Select **Screen Time.**
3. Scroll to the **Family** section, then tap the desired family member.
4. Select **Content & Privacy Restrictions.**

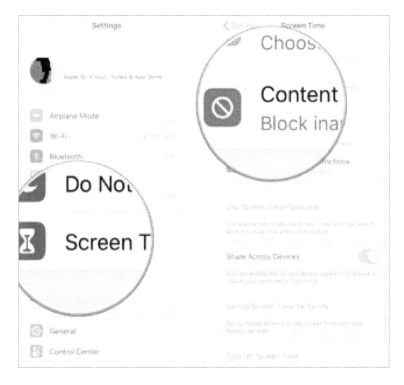

5. Select **Content Restrictions.**

6. Then click on **Apps.**

7. Choose the highest rating that should be allowed on the iPhone. Alternatively, select **Allow All Apps** or **Don't Allow Apps.**

Block Adding Friends from Game Center

To prevent your kids from adding new friends from the game center, use the guide below:

1. Launch the **Settings** app.
2. Select **Screen Time.**
3. Select **Content & Privacy Restrictions.**
4. Select **Content Restrictions.**
5. Select **Adding Friends.**
6. Then tap **Don't Allow.**

Block Multiplayer Games from the Game Center

1. Launch the **Settings** app.
2. Select **Screen Time**.
3. Select **Content & Privacy Restrictions.**

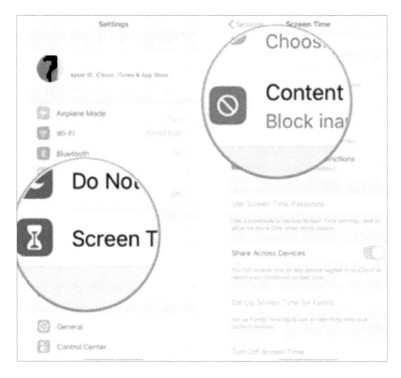

4. Select **Content Restrictions.**

5. Then tap **Multiplayer Games.**

6. Click on **Don't Allow.**

Prevent Screen Recording

1. Launch the **Settings** app.
2. Select **Screen Time**.
3. Select **Content & Privacy Restrictions.**
4. Select **Content Restrictions.**
5. Select **Screen Recording.**
6. Then click on **Don't Allow.**

Chapter 10: Control Center

In the Control Center of your iPhone SE, you can control, access and customize features and apps like torchlight, music playback, Bluetooth, QR scanner and so on.

Access Control Center

This is a quick way to access control center on your device:

1. Place your finger at the bottom edge of your screen, then swipe up to the top of the screen to view the control center.
2. Press on the home button to exit the control center.

Enable Control Center on Your Lock Screen

Would you like to be able to access the control center on a locked screen? Then follow the steps below:

1. Select **Touch ID and Passcode** within the **Settings** app.
2. Type your phone's passcode when prompted.
3. Go down to **Control Center,** move the switch to the left to disable or to the right to enable.

Disable Access to Control Center from Within Apps

You can access control center even when using apps on your phone. But if you do not want to be able to access control center from within apps, follow the steps below to disable it:

1. Launch the **Settings** app.
2. Select **Control Center.**
3. Go to **Access Within Apps,** move the switch to the left to disable or to the right to enable.

Customize Control Center

By customizing your control center, you can add your frequently used apps and remove the apps you do not use often.

1. Select **Control Center** within the **Settings** app.
2. Select **Customize Controls.**
3. Tap ⊖ beside the apps you want to remove, then tap **Remove** to delete the controls.
4. Tap ⊕ beside the controls you want to add.

Rearrange Controls in the Control Center

1. Select **Control Center** within the Settings app.
2. Select **Customize Controls.**
3. Tap and hold the ☰ icon beside the controls you want to rearrange, then drag that to arrange them in the order that you like.

Modify Access to Items on Locked Screen

The iPhone SE has some features and apps that you can access on the control center when your device is locked. You can customize these items to view the ones that you use often.

1. Select **Touch ID and Passcode** within the **Settings** app.
2. On the next screen, go through the list and enable or disable the apps that you do not want to access on locked screen.

Chapter 11: Apple Maps

Apple updated their Maps app to include features such as sharing estimated arrival time with other people, collections (allows you to create lists of local interesting spaces and spots), keep track of special locations, and so much more. In this section, we will explore the features of the Apple Maps.

Share Your ETA

When you share your ETA with family and friends, they can view your estimated time of arrival on a trip, or any changes that occur during that trip.

1. Launch the Apple **Maps.**
2. Search for your destination in the search bar, or select your destination from your **Favorite** or **Recently Viewed** to bring up an address fast.
3. Click on **Directions** to start your journey. Don't forget to select your

means of transportation, whether **Walk, Ride, Drive,** or **Transit.**

4. Tap **Go** to begin your journey.

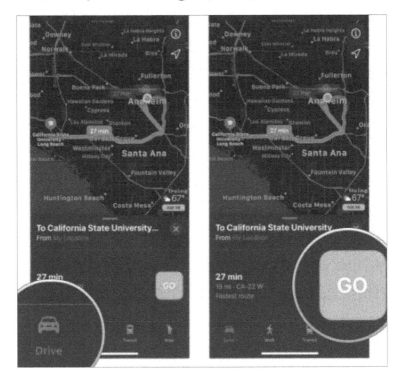

5. Navigate to the bottom of the screen and click on **Share ETA.**

6. Click on the contact you wish to share your movement with.

View Another Person's ETA

You will receive a notification on your phone whenever someone shares their ETA with you. You can view and get live updates on their trip.

1. Select the ETA notification to take you directly to Apple **Maps.**
2. On the map, you will see their journey and the estimated time of arrival.

Stop Sharing ETA

Follow the steps below to stop sharing your ETA:

1. Open the **Maps** app still showing directions.
2. At the bottom of the screen, tap **Sharing ETA with X (number) people.**
3. Select the contact whom you no longer wish to share your ETA with.

4. Your phone will instantly stop sharing your ETA with that person.

Create Favorite Locations

If you frequent a place like your office address, you may Favorite the address to have the address always show at the top of the Maps screen. You can also view the estimated time of arrival for your favorited locations. Follow the steps below to add a location to your Favorite bar:

1. Launch the **Maps** app.
2. Pull up the search bar indent until the map is no longer showing (please refer to screenshot).
3. Go to the Favorite section and tap **Add.**

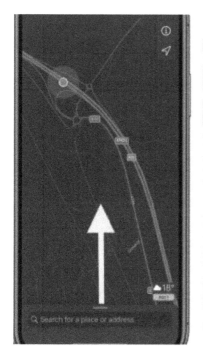

4. Type the address or name of the place you want to favorite. To search using your voice, tap the Siri icon and call out the name or address.

5. Look for the address under **Suggestions,** then tap the  icon to add that address to your Favorites.

6. On the next screen, tap **Label** if you wish to change the name of the place.

7. Under **Type,** choose your preferred option that best describes the place.

8. Click on **Add Person,** under **Share ETA** to share your journey to this location with your contact.
9. Tap **Done** to complete set up.

Delete Favorite

Follow the steps below to remove an address from your Favorites:

1. From the home screen of the Apple **Maps**, tap **See All** (beside **Favorites**).
2. Click on the  icon beside the saved location you want to delete.
3. Then select **Remove Favorite** at the bottom of your screen.

Create Collections in the Map

Create a collection of places in your desired destination to help you keep track of, even before you reach your destination. For instance, if you plan to visit Florida and you also want to take the kids to Disney World while there, you can create a Collection for Florida, then add all the places you will like to visit while in Florida. Follow the steps below to create a collection:

1. From the **Maps** home screen, drag up the handle at the bottom to expand the panel.
2. From Collections, click on **New Collections.**
3. Choose a name for your Collection then tap **Create.**
4. Your Collection is ready.

Add Addresses to Your Collections

Follow the steps below to add addresses to Collections that you created:

1. Click on the new collection you just created.
2. Navigate to the bottom of your screen and tap **Add a Place.**
3. Type the address, place or landmark you want to visit.
4. Click  beside the desired location under **Suggestions.** To add other

addresses, just clear the search bar and type the new address or place, and click  again beside the new address.

5. Tap **Done** once you finish adding all the places to your Collection.

Delete an Address from Your Collections

To remove an address, place or location from your collections, follow the steps below:

1. Launch the Apple **Maps**.
2. Tap a collection to open it.
3. Navigate to the bottom of your screen and click on **Edit.**
4. Select the addresses or places you want to delete.
5. Tap **Delete** to remove the addresses or locations from that Collection.

Explore Your Collection Locations

1. To know more about a location in your Collections, click on the address.

2. Click on **Directions** to see how you can get to that location.

3. Tap **Flyover** to have a close look at the area.

4. To add a location to your Favorite, click on the location, scroll down and tap **Add to Favorite.**

5. Click on **Report an Issue** if you find anything amiss about the location.

6. To add this location to another Collection, tap **Add** at the top of your screen.

7. Select **Share** to send the details of this location to family or friends via messaging apps.

Chapter 12: Apple Notes App

The Apple Note app allows you to store your information and data on your iPhone SE. You can make your jottings, lists, and other important information there. You can also create a password for your Notes to prevent third party access.

Create Password for Notes in The Settings App

1. Launch the **Settings** app.
2. Tap **Notes.**

3. Select **Password.**
4. Type in your desired password.
5. Re-type the password again.
6. Type in a hint in case you forget the password.
7. Enable **Touch ID** by toggling on the switch to the right if you want to be able to open locked Notes using your registered fingerprint.
8. Tap **Done** and you have successfully created a Password for your notes.

Create Password for Notes in the Notes App

When you try to lock a note for the first time, a prompt will appear on your screen requesting you to set a global password for locking your notes. If you choose to be proactive and create a password immediately, follow the steps below:

1. Launch the **Notes** app.

2. Click on an existing note or create a new note.

3. Select the **Share** button

4. Then select **Lock Note.**

5. Type in your desired password.
6. Re-type the password again.

7. Type in a hint in case you forget the password.
8. Enable **Touch ID** by toggling on the switch to the right if you want to be able to open locked Notes using your registered fingerprint.
9. Tap **Done** and you have successfully created a Password for your notes.

Reset Notes Password

If you are unable to remember the password you created for the Note app and you did not activate Touch ID for Notes, follow the steps below to reset the password:

1. Open the **Settings** app.
2. Select **Notes.**
3. Select **Password.**

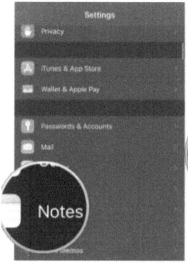

4. Select **Reset Password.**

5. Enter your iCloud password.

6. Click on **OK.**

7. Tap **Reset Password.**

8. Enter a new password.

9. Re-enter the new password.

10. Fill in the space for password hint.
11. Turn on the switch for **Touch ID.**
12. Tap **Done.**

Change Notes Password
1. Open the **Settings** app.
2. Select **Notes.**
3. Select **Password.**
4. Click on **Change Password.**
5. Type your current password.
6. Type your new password.
7. Re-type the new password.
8. Fill in the space for password hint.
9. Tap **Done.**

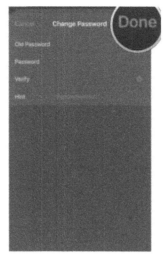

Lock a Note Using Your Password or Touch ID

Here is how to lock the notes that you do not want others to see:

1. Launch the **Notes** app.
2. Click on an existing note or create a new note.

3. Select the **Share** button
4. Then select **Lock Note.**

5. Select **Touch ID** and place your finger on the home button to lock it. Or tap **Enter Password** and type in your Notes password.
6. Click **Ok.**
7. You will see a lock button on your screen to confirm that the note has been locked.
8. This will only lock the content of the note. People can still see the title of the note. Ensure not to include sensitive details in your title.

Unlock Your Note

1. From the **Notes** app, tap on the locked note.
2. Select **View Note** (middle of screen), or click on the lock icon (at the top of your screen).

3. Place your registered finger on the home button to unlock the note, or type in your password.

Relock a Note

The Notes app is designed to automatically relock a locked app when you close the Notes app, reboot your phone, lock your phone or restart the

Notes app. However, follow the steps below to manually relock any note:

1. Launch the **Notes** app.
2. Select the note you plan to relock.
3. Select the **Lock** icon  at the top of your screen.

4. You will instantly receive a notification that the note has been locked.

Chapter 13: Reminders

The Reminders app enables you to receive an alert whilst messaging someone, set alerts that are based on location and time, and create reminders that includes attachments and subtasks. These and more are some of the things you can do on the Reminders app.

Create a Reminder

Follow the steps below to create a new reminder:

1. Launch the **Reminders** app.

2. Select an existing list.
3. Scroll to the bottom of your screen and tap **New Reminder.**

4. Type your reminder into the text field.
5. Then tap **Done.**

Tag Someone in Your Reminder

You may tag someone when creating a reminder so that when next you are messaging that person; you will receive an alert to notify you of your reminder.

1. Launch the **Reminders** app.
2. Select an existing list.
3. Scroll to the bottom of your screen and tap **New Reminder.**
4. Type your reminder in the text field.
5. Tap the  button on the new reminder to view the Details screen.
6. Go to **Remind Me When Messaging** and move the switch to the right to enable the option.

7. Tap **Choose Person** to select a contact. If you already added someone to the reminder, tap **Edit** to make your changes.
8. Select **Done.**
9. When next you want to send a message to the contact, you will receive a reminder on your screen and in the Notification center until you complete the reminder.

Add an Attachment to a Reminder

Now you have created your reminder, follow the steps below to add an attachment to the reminder

1. Launch the **Reminders** app.
2. Select an existing list.
3. Scroll to the bottom of your screen and tap **New Reminder.**
4. Type your reminder in the text field.
5. Tap the camera icon 📷 on top of your keyboard.

6. Choose your best option from the displayed list: scan a document, take a new photo, etc.
7. Tap **Done** to complete the reminder.

Share a Reminder

Follow the steps below to share your reminder with family and friends:

1. Launch the **Reminders** app.
2. Select the list you plan to share.
3. Tap the ⬤ icon at the top right side of your screen.
4. A drop-down list will appear on your screen. Tap **Add People.**
5. Enter your receiver's address and tap **Add.**
6. Then tap **Done.**

Create a New List

To create a new list:

1. Launch the **Reminders** app.

2. Navigate to the bottom of the app's home screen and click on **Add List.**

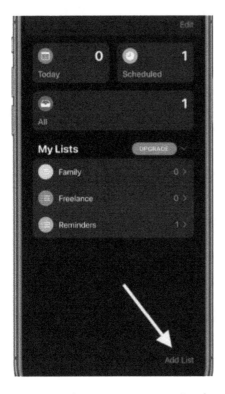

3. Give your reminder a name.
4. Choose a color and an icon to differentiate your list.
5. Tap **Done.**

Edit a List

Follow the steps below to edit an existing list:

1. Open the **Reminders** app and select the list you plan to edit.
2. Tap the 3-dot icon ⋯ at the top of your screen.
3. Tap **Name and Appearance.**

4. Proceed to change the name, the color or the icon of the list.

5. Tap **Done** to confirm your changes.

Delete a List

Here is how to delete a list you no longer want:

1. Launch the **Reminders** app.

2. Scroll to the list you want to delete, and swipe left on it.

3. Select the  icon.

Move a Reminder to a Different List

There are two ways to relocate a reminder to another list:

Method 1

1. Launch the **Reminders** app.
2. Select the list where the reminder is saved in.
3. Select the reminder.
4. Then click the ⓘ button.
5. Tap **List** and choose the new list you plan to move the reminder to.
6. Tap **Done.**

Method 2

1. Tap the reminder you want to move and hold it with one finger.
2. Use another finger to tap the list button to take you back to your list.
3. Go to the new list you plan to place the reminder in and release the finger holding the reminder you want to move. This will drop the reminder in the new list.

Create a Scheduled Reminder

Follow the steps below to create a scheduled reminder:

1. Launch the **Reminders** app.
2. Select the list that you plan to create a scheduled reminder in.
3. Select **New Reminder** at the bottom of your screen.
4. Give a name to your reminder.
5. Then tap ⓘ by the side of the reminder name.
6. Go to **Remind me On a Day** and move the switch to the right to enable it.
7. Tap **Alarm** and choose your desired date.
8. If you will like the app to give you a reminder at a specified time and date, go to **Remind Me at a Time,** then select the time you will like to receive the alert.
9. Tap **Done.**

View Completed Reminders

Whenever you complete a task, the reminder for that task automatically leaves the home screen of the reminder app to make it easy for you to access other active reminders. However, the steps below will guide you on how to show completed reminders in your app home screen.

1. Launch the **Reminders** app.
2. Go to **My Lists** and tap on a list.
3. Tap the ⋯ icon at the top right side of your screen.

4. You will see a drop-down menu on your screen, select **Show Completed** to view your completed reminders. If you no longer want to see the completed reminders, come back to this step and click on **Hide Completed.**

Group Different Lists Together

You can bring together similar lists into one group. For instance, combine all your shopping lists into one group and term the group **Personal Shopping** group. Follow the steps below to do this:

1. Launch the **Reminders** app.
2. Tap **Edit** at the top right side of your screen.
3. Navigate to the bottom of your screen and click **Add Group.**

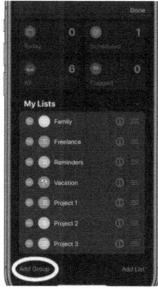

4. Name your group.
5. To add lists to the new group, tap **Include** and click on the lists that should go into the group.

6. Select the **New Group** back icon to return to the previous screen.
7. Select **Create** and your group is ready.

Delete a Group

Here is how to delete a group in your reminder app:

1. Launch the **Reminders** app.
2. Scroll to the group you want to delete, and swipe left on it.
3. Tap the 🗑 icon.
4. A pop-up will appear on your screen with multiple options. Tap **Delete Group Only** to delete the group but retain the lists in the group. Tap **Delete Group and Lists** to remove the group and the lists in the group.

Change Reminder Priority

Here is how to set a priority for your reminder:

1. Launch the **Reminders** app.
2. Click on a list to open it.
3. Then tap the reminder.
4. Scroll to the bottom of your screen and tap **Priority.**
5. The next screen will display multiple priority options for you. Click on your preference.

6. Tap the **Details** back button to go back.

7. Then tap **Done.**

Flag a Reminder

When you flag a reminder, the reminder automatically goes to the **Flagged** smart list on the app's home screen for easy viewing each time you launch the app. There are two ways to flag a reminder:

Method 1

1. Launch the **Reminders** app.
2. Click on a list to open it.
3. Then tap the reminder you want to flag.
4. Tap the ⚑ icon on top your keyboard. To unflag, tap the ⚑ icon again.

Method 2

1. Launch the **Reminders** app.
2. Click on a list to open it.
3. Then tap the reminder you want to flag.
4. Tap the ⓘ icon, then go to the **Flagged** option and move the switch to the right or to the left to flag or unflag.

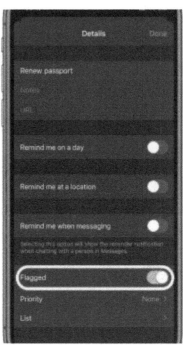

Chapter 14: Files App

The Files App on your iPhone SE is where your documents are saved. The App allows you to do several things like share a document with others, invite colleagues to collaborate on a document, and lots more.

Share a Document for Collaboration

You can share a document with a colleague or friend that has an iPhone and also uses iCloud. Here is how to:

1. Launch the **Files** app.

2. Select **iCloud Drive.**

3. Select the folder that contains the document you plan to share.

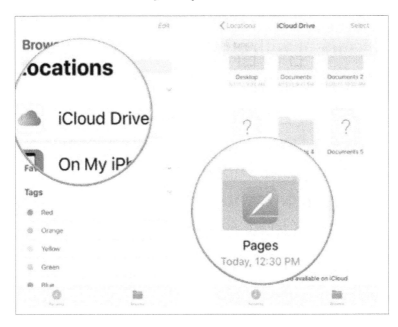

4. Tap **Select** at the top right side of your screen.

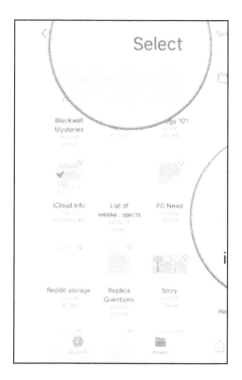

5. Choose the document you want to collaborate on.

6. Then click the 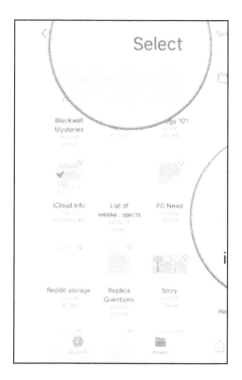 icon.

7. In the Share Sheet, select **Add People.**

8. Click on the method you want to use to invite others for collaboration.

9. Choose a contact.

10.   Click **Send.**

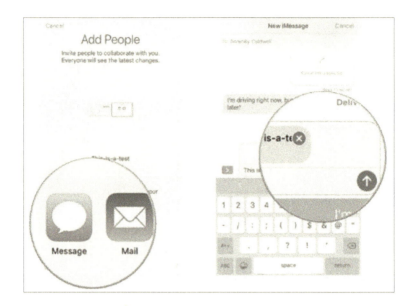

Adjust Permissions for a Document in iCloud

You can choose to give some people the right to edit a document while making it view-only for others. Follow the steps below to modify the permissions for everyone or for each invitee:

1. From the **Files** app, tap **iCloud Drive.**
2. Select the folder that contains the document you are collaborating on.

3. Tap **Select** at the top right side of your screen.
4. Choose the document for which you plan to alter the permissions.
5. Then click the 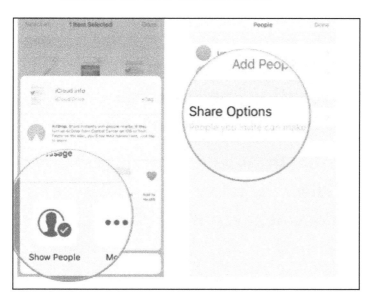 icon.
6. In the Share Sheet, select **Show People.**
7. Select **Share Options** to alter permissions for everyone who has access to the document.

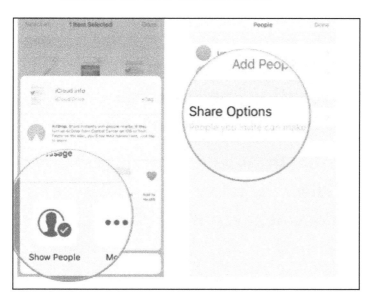

8. Click on a **Contact** to modify the permission for that person.

9. You will see two permission settings on the next screen. Click on the one you want to assign to that person.

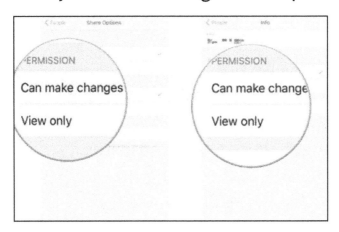

Remove Someone from Collaborating in a Document

Here is how to un-invite collaborators:

1. From the **Files** app, tap **iCloud Drive.**
2. Select the folder that has the document you want to change.

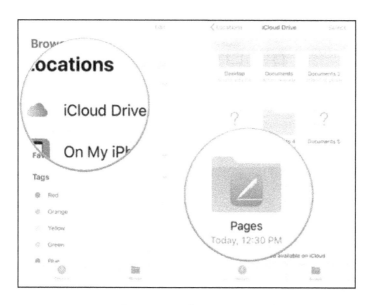

3. Tap **Select** at the top right area of your screen.
4. Choose the document you want to adjust.
5. Then click the ⬆️ icon.
6. In the Share Sheet, select **Show People.**
7. Select the contact you want to stop collaborating with.
8. Click **Remove Access.**

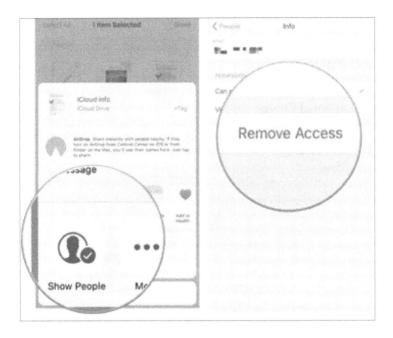

9. Select **Ok** to confirm your action.

10. If you invited several people to collaborate on a document and you wish to un-invite all the participants, select **Stop Sharing** at the lower corner of your invite list.

Chapter 15: Find My

Find My in iPhone SE combines the functions of the previous Find My Friends app and the Find My iPhone app. The app allows you to find your missing device, erase lost device, share your location with others, etc.

Find Friends in 'Find My'

Follow the steps below to view the current location of your friends:

1. Open the **Find My app.**

2. Go to the **People tab** if you are not on that view already.

3. On the map, you will be able to view the locations of people who are sharing their location with you. Click on the person you wish to see their location.

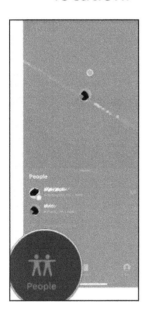

4. Swipe up on that card you want to access, then tap **Contact** to show you the details of that contact.

5. Tap **Directions** to be directed to their present location.
6. Tap **Edit Location Name** if you wish to modify the name of their present location.
7. Tap **Add (followed by the contacts name)** to add the contact to Favorites.
8. To add a label to your contact's present location, click on **Label,** then tap **Add Custom Label.**

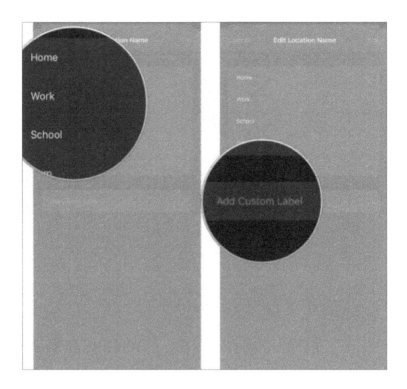

Share Your Location

Enable this option to be able to share your location with others.

1. Click on the **Me** tab in the **Find My** app home screen.
2. Go to **Share My Location** and move the switch to the right to enable, or to the left to disable sharing.

Add Friends in Find My

The steps below will guide you on how to add other Apple users to your Find My:

1. Click on the **People** tab in the **Find My** app home screen.
2. Tap **Share My Location.**

3. Enter in the name of the contact you want to add, or select the contact from the list.

4. Select  to add more people.

5. Click **Send.**
6. Choose the sharing duration from the list on your screen.

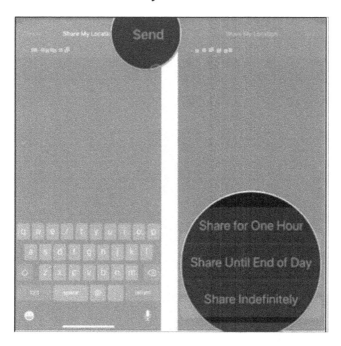

Notify Friends of Your Location

1. Click on the **People** tab in the **Find My** app home screen.
2. On the map, select a contact who is sharing their current location with you.

3. Swipe up and then select **Add** in the
   Notifications tab.
4. Tap **Notify (followed by the name of
   the contact).**
5. Choose your preferred option on the
   next screen: **When I leave** or **When I
   Arrive.**

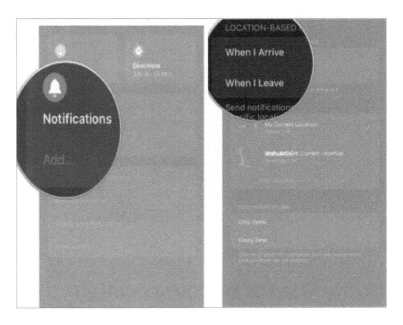

6. Select a location from the map or tap
   Add Location to create another
   location that is not on the list.
7. Choose how often you want the
   contact to be alerted on your

notification: **Every Time** or **Only Once.**

8. Tap **Add.**

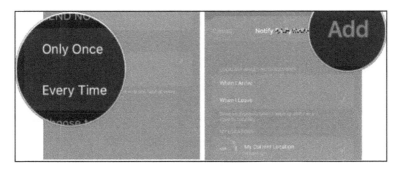

Stop Sharing Your Location

1. Click on the **People** tab in the **Find My** app home screen.
2. On the map, tap a contact who is currently sharing their location with you.
3. Swipe up and select **Stop Sharing My Location.**
4. Then select **Stop Sharing Location.**

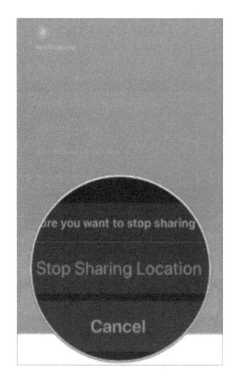

5. If you want to remove the contact from your friend list, tap **Remove (then the contact's name).**

6. Then tap **Remove.**

Find Devices

1. Click on the **Devices** tab in the **Find My** app home screen.
2. Select the device that you want to find.
3. Swipe up and select the desired button or switch, either **Mark as Lost** (to declare a device as missing), **Play Sound** (to make a sound when looking for your device nearby), **Directions** (to show you the way to your device's present location), or **Notifications** (to receive a

notification whenever your device is
found).

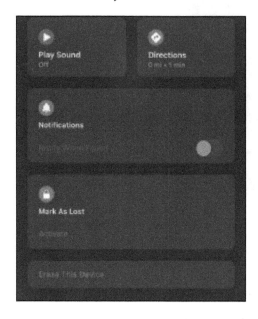

Mark a Device as Lost

1. Click on the **Device** tab in the **Find
   My** app home screen.
2. Select the missing device.
3. Swipe up, go to **Mark as Lost** and
   select **Activate.**
4. Tap **Continue.**

5. Alternatively, you can type your phone number in the phone number field if you want.

6. Tap **Next.**

7. Type a message for whoever comes across the phone.

8. Tap **Activate** to lock your phone. The only way to unlock the phone now is to enter your passcode.

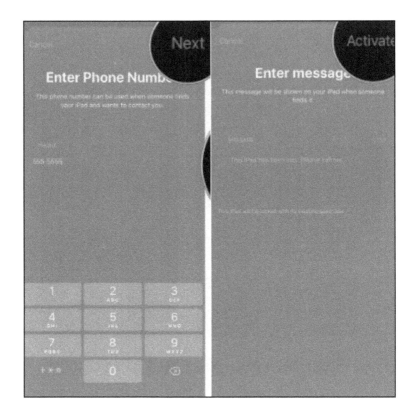

Remotely Erase a Device

1. Click on the **Device** tab in the **Find My** app home screen.
2. Select the missing device.
3. Swipe up, and select **Erase This Device.**
4. Click on **Erase This** (followed by the device name).

5. Alternatively, you can type your phone number in the phone number field if you want.

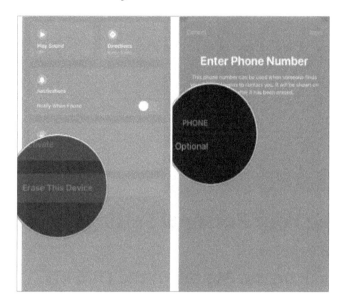

6. Tap **Next.**
7. Type a message for whoever comes across the phone.
8. Tap **Erase** to wipe your phone.

Manage Your Personal Settings in Find My

1. Click on the **Me** tab in the **Find My** app home screen.
2. Swipe up, to display your options.
3. Toggle on or off the switch for **Share My Location.**

4. Switch on or off the option for **Allow Friends Request** as desired.

5. Select **Receive Location Updates** to choose people who should receive notifications on your location.

6. Click on your preferred option from the displayed list.

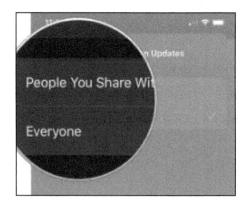

7. Tap the **Me** back arrow to return to the previous screen.
8. Select **Edit Location Name.**

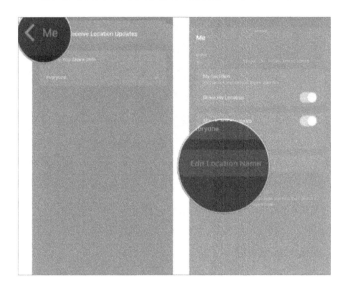

9. Tap **Label** and choose the one that best suits the location.
10.   Select **Add Custom Label** to set up custom label for the different locations.

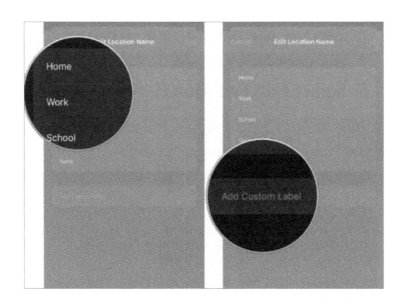

Chapter 16: Camera and Photos

The camera of your iPhone SE allows you to take awesome still photos and great video footages. We will explore the amazing features of the iPhone SE camera in this chapter.

Enhance Images in Photos

1. Launch the **Photos** app.
2. Tap the photo you wish to enhance.
3. Tap **Edit** at the top of your screen.
4. Go to the bottom of the screen and tap the **Auto-Enhance** button
5. Turn the dial to the right or to the left side to adjust the intensity of the image.
6. Tap **Done** to confirm your changes or tap **Cancel** to discard the changes.

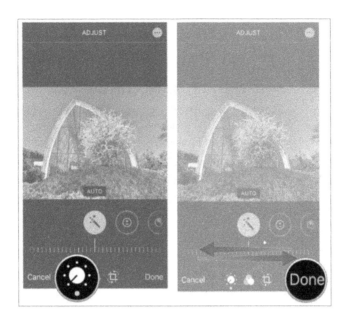

Change Lighting in your Photos

To manually change the lighting on your photos, follow the steps below:

1. Launch the **Photos** app.
2. Tap the picture you want to adjust.
3. Tap **Edit** at the top of the screen.
4. Go to the bottom of the screen and tap the **Auto-Enhance** button

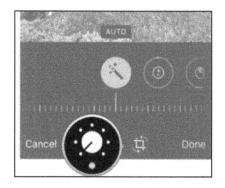

5. Swipe horizontally on the different menus and tap each category and adjust as needed.

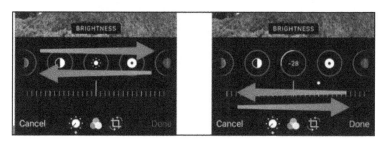

6. When you make any adjustment, slide the ![icon] icon to get a stronger or weaker effect.

7. When you finish, tap **Done** to complete.

Adjust Color in Your Photos

Follow the steps below to modify the colors of your image.

1. Launch the **Photos** app.
2. Tap a photo to launch it.
3. Tap **Edit.**
4. Tap the 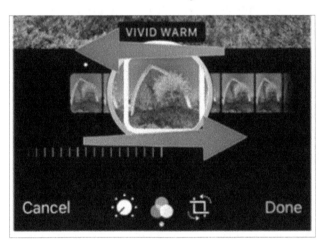 button at the bottom of your screen.
5. Move left and right until you get a color filter that your desire.

6. Slide the icon for a stronger or weaker effect.
7. Then swipe to the left and right to try the four available options: **Tint, Warmth, Vibrance,** and **Saturation.**

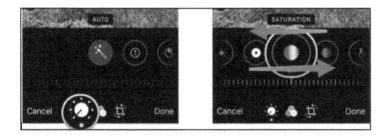

8. Slide the 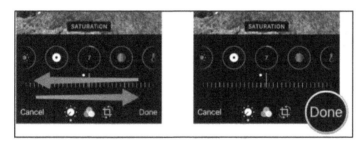dial for each of the four available options till you get a look that you like.

9. When you finish, tap **Done** to complete.

Convert Photos to Black and White

Here is how to change your photo to Black and White:

1. Launch the **Photos** app.
2. Tap a photo to launch it.
3. Tap **Edit.**

4. Tap the ⬤ button at the bottom of your screen.

5. Move left and right until you get to the three black and white filters: **Noir, Mono**, and **Silvertone**. When you get to each category, your image will automatically reflect the new color.

6. Slide the 🎛 dial to modify the selected lighting aspect till you get a look that you like.

7. When you finish, tap **Done** to complete.

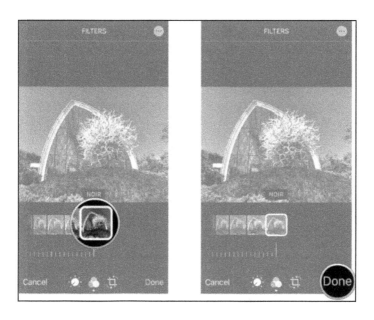

Revert to the Original Photo

So, you made changes to a photo and have saved the changes but will like to revert to the original photo? Here is how you can achieve this:

1. Click on the edited photo in the **Photos** app.
2. Tap **Edit.**
3. Click **Revert.**

4. Then select **Revert to Original** and the image will return to its original look.

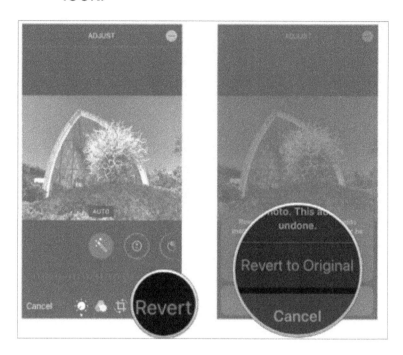

Find Memories in Photo

The operating system of the iPhone SE is designed in a way that it creates memories using pictures stored in the Photo app. Follow the steps below to find memories in the Photo app:

1. From the **Photos** app, select the **For You** tab.
2. Scroll to the Memories section and select **See All.**
3. Click on the memory you want to access.

Search for Memories

Let's say you saw a memory that you liked but you have so many memories and not able to easily get to the one you want to view. This is an easy step to search for memories in the Photo app:

1. Click the **Search** bar in the **Photos** app home screen.
2. Type in the keyword or search term for the memory you want to bring up.
3. Select the memory from the search results.

Start a Slideshow in Memories

You can convert your memories into a slideshow with the steps below:

1. From the **Photos** app, select the **For You** tab.
2. Scroll to the Memories section and select **See All.**
3. Click on the memory you want to access.
4. Tap the ▶ button on the cover of the memory to start the slideshow.

Change Your Slideshow Theme

You can change the theme of a slideshow with the steps below:

1. Follow the steps above to play the memory.
2. Then tap on any part of your screen while the memory is playing.
3. Tap the ❚❚ button to pause the slideshow.
4. Move down to the menu bar and swipe to the left or the right to view

different themes. Click on the theme that you like. Each theme has its own different font face and background song.

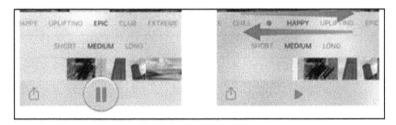

5. When you find the theme that you like, tap it to apply it to your slideshow.
6. Tap the ▶ button at the bottom of your screen to continue playing your slideshow.

Edit Your Memories During Slideshow

You can make the memories slideshow shorter, change the music, remove or add photos to the memories as well as edit the title.

1. After changing the theme of the slideshow, under the Theme menu bar is the **Duration** option. There are three duration options: Short, which is 31 seconds. Medium, which is 1 min and 1 sec. Long, which is 1 min and 20 sec. Choose the length that suits you.

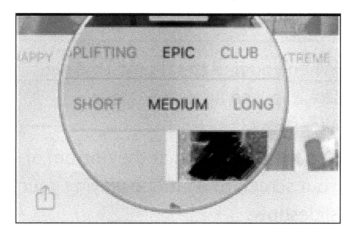

2. Once done, scroll up and tap **Edit** at the top of your screen.
3. You will see different options pop up on your screen, like Duration, Title, Image etc. Click on the one that you want to change.

4. Make the necessary changes and tap **Done** to complete.

Delete Photos from a Memories Slideshow

Memories bring together different pictures taken in different locations with different people. Follow the steps below to delete a picture from a memory.

1. After changing the theme of the slideshow, scroll up and tap **Edit** at the top of your screen.
2. You will see different options pop up on your screen, like Duration, Title, Image etc. Tap **Photos & Videos.**

3. Scroll through the timeline of the video until you find the picture you want to delete.

4. Select  icon to delete the image from the slideshow. Do not fret. The image will not be deleted from your library.

5. After removing the images that you do not want, tap **Done** to save.

6. Tap **Done** again to complete the action.

Save a Memories Slideshow

After editing and modifying your slideshow, the steps below will show you how to save the slideshow:

1. Follow the steps above to edit your slideshow.

2. Once done, tap the ⬆ icon at the bottom of your screen.

3. Look through the Share Sheet and tap **Save Video.**

Favorite a Memories Slideshow

Follow the steps below to add a slideshow to your Favorite list:

1. From the **Photos** app, select the **For You** tab.
2. Scroll to the Memories section and select **See All.**
3. Click on the memory you want to access.
4. Tap the ⬤ icon at the top of your phone screen.
5. Now tap **Add to Favorite Memories.**

View Your Favorite Memories

After you have successfully added a memory to your Favorites, follow the steps below to view your Favorite list:

1. From the **Photos** app, select the **For You** tab.
2. Scroll to the Memories section and select **See All.**
3. Tap **Favorites** and all the videos you favorited will be displayed on your screen.

Delete a Memory

Did Apple create a memory that you do not want to keep? The steps below will show you how to delete it:

1. From the **Photos** app, select the **For You** tab.
2. Scroll to the Memories section and select **See All.**

3. Tap the memory that you want to delete.

4. Tap the  icon at the top of your phone screen.

5. Now tap **Delete Memory.**

See Who Was in Your Memories

So, you desire to know the people that featured in your Memories? This is how to do this:

1. From the **Photos** app, select the **For You** tab.

2. Scroll to the Memories section and select **See All.**

3. Tap the memory that you want to view.

4. Scroll to the **Groups and People** section, then move to the left and to the right to see all the people that showed in your memories.

See Where Your Memories Happened on a Map

1. From the **Photos** app, select the **For You** tab.
2. Scroll to the Memories section and select **See All.**
3. Tap the memory that you want to view.
4. Scroll to the **Places** section, and click on the map to view the location where the photos were shot.
5. Select **Show Nearby Photos** to view all the photos that you shot in one location, including images that are not in the present slideshow.

Share a Memory

1. From the **Photos** app, select the **For You** tab.
2. Scroll to the Memories section and select **See All.**
3. Tap the memory that you want to view.
4. With the movie playing, click the 📤 icon and click on the method for sharing the video.

Share Photos or Videos

Follow the steps below to share an image or photo on your photo app.

1. From the **Photos** app, select the video or photo you want to share.
2. Click the 📤 icon and click on the method for sharing the video or photo.

Share Multiple Videos or Photos

Here is a guide to share more than one image:

1. Launch the **Photos** app.
2. Go to the top of your screen and tap **Select.**
3. Tap all the videos or photos you want to send out.
4. Click the  icon and decide on the method for sharing the videos or photos.

Print Photos

1. From the **Photos** app, tap the image you want to print.

2. Click the  icon at the bottom of your screen.

3. Tap **Print** from the available options.

4. Click **Select Printer** and set up your printer.

5. Tap the $-$ or $+$ icons to input number of copies you want.

6. Tap **Print** to print the image.

Shoot Video with your iPhone

Here is how to shoot videos on your SE:

1. Launch the **Camera** app.
2. You can either tap **Videos** at the bottom of your screen or swipe to the right to enter the Video mode.

3. Tap ⭕ to begin shooting your video.
4. Once done, tap ⬛button to stop recording.
5. Your video will now save in the Photo Library.

Save Live Photos as a Video

1. From the **Photos** app, tap the Live Photo you want to convert to Video. You will see the ▣ LIVE tag beside every Live Photo.

2. Click the ⬆ icon and tap **Save as Video.**

3. The video will automatically save in the **Recents** album.

Find All Live Photos Fast

You might be unable to separate the Live Photos from the regular photos by just taking a simple glance in your camera roll. The good news is that the Live photos have their own album. Follow the steps below to find this album and also save the Live Photos as video.

1. From the **Photos** app, select **Albums.**

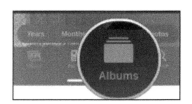

2. Tap **Live Photos** under **Media Types.**

3. Scroll up and tap **Select.**

4. Choose the Live Photos you plan to use for the video.

5. Click the  icon and tap **Save as Video.**

6. The video will automatically save in the **Recents** album.

Change Video Resolution and Frame Rate

The iPhone SE camera can be used to shoot 4K videos on 24fps to 60 fps. Follow the steps below to change your video resolution and frame rate.

1. From the **Settings** app, tap **Camera.**
2. Select **Record Video.**

3. Then choose your desired video resolution and frame rate.

Shoot Slo-mo Video

After shooting a high FPS (i.e. frames per second) video, you can return to the recording to reduce the speed or increase the speed of any parts of the recording.

1. Launch the **Camera** app and tap **Slo-mo.** Alternatively, if you are in the Photos mode, swipe right two times to go into the slow motion mode.

2. Tap to start recording.

3. Tap to stop recording.

Modify the Normal and Slow Speed Points for Slo-Mo Videos

When you are done shooting your videos as slo-mo, you can now follow the steps below to increase the speed or reduce the speed of any desired part of the video.

1. Launch the **Photos** app and select the slo-mo video.

2. Another way to access Slo-mo videos is to go to **Albums** in the Photos app, tap **Slo-mo,** then tap the video you want to edit.

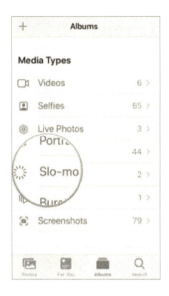

Media Types

◻ Videos	6 >
▣ Selfies	65 >
◎ Live Photos	3 >
Porti...	44 >
Slo-mo	2 >
Bur...	1 >
◉ Screenshots	79 >

3. Tap **Edit** at the top right of your screen to display the video timeline.

4. Click and pull the slider at both ends of the screen to choose when the video should go in and out of slow motion.

5. Tap **Done** and your Slo-mo video is ready.

6. To return the video back to its original format, come to step five and tap **Revert.**

Switch Between 120 fps and 240 fps Slo-mo

You have the option of recording your Slo-mo videos at 720p at 240 fps or 1080p at 120 fps. Follow the steps below to set up your preferred option for shooting slow motion videos.

1. From the **Settings** app, tap **Camera.**
2. Tap **Record Slo-mo.**
3. Then select your preferred shooting option.

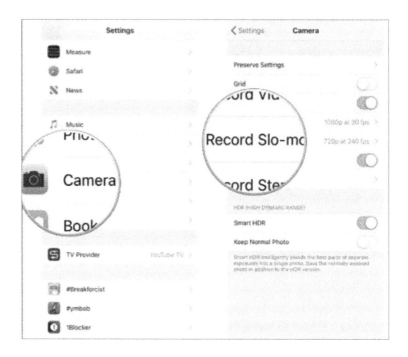

Create Time Lapse Video

Shoot this video to show the amount of time that passed since you started recording. To get the best result, let your phone be on landscape mode and also use a tripod.

1. Launch the **Camera** app.
2. Swipe to the right of your screen three times. Another way to get to the Time Lapse view is to click on

Time Lapse after you make the first swipe.

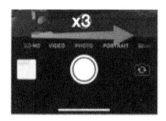

3. Tap to begin shooting your video.
4. Once done, tap button to stop recording.
5. You get best results when you shoot a long video.

Take a Still Photo while Capturing Video

Do you know that you can take a picture while shooting a video? Follow the steps below:

1. From the home screen of the **Camera** app, swipe to the right to get into the Video mode.

2. Tap  to begin shooting your video.

3. While the video recording is on, tap the white button beside the Red button to capture your photo.

Edit Videos

Here is how you can edit videos on your iPhone SE:

1. Launch the **Photos** app and tap the video you plan to edit.

2. Select **Edit** at the top right side of your screen.

3. Scroll to the bottom of your screen to view different editing tools.
4. Click on each button and edit as you wish.

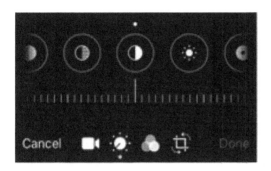

5. Tap **Done** to accept the modification or tap **Cancel** to discard the changes.

Change Wallpaper from the Photos App

1. Launch the **Photos** app and tap the image you want for your wallpaper.

2. Click the ⬆️ icon and tap **Use as Wallpaper.**

3. You will see a prompt on your screen to choose between **Live, Perspective, or Still Image.**

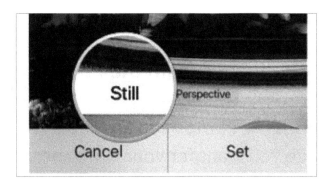

4. Tap **Set.**

5. You will receive a pop-up menu on your screen. Select the option you prefer.

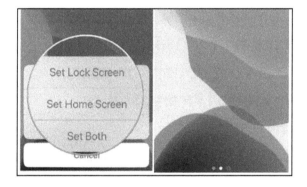

Change Your Wallpaper

This is how to change your wallpaper:

1. Click on **Wallpaper** in the **Settings** app.

2. Select **Choose a New Wallpaper.**

3. Select the type of wallpaper you want from the options on your screen: **Photo Library, Still,** or **Dynamic.**

   o Tap **Photo Library** to select an image from your photo library.

   o Click on **Still** if you want a non-changing photo from Apple's photo library.

- Click on **Dynamic Wallpaper** to get your images (that has effects) from Apple's photo library.

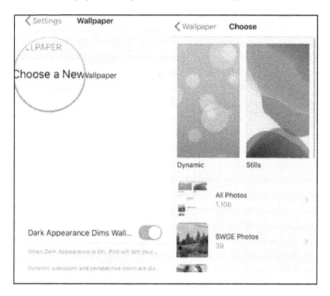

4. Tap a photo to go to Preview mode.
5. Move the photo around your screen until you are able to get the desired fit.
6. Tap **Set.**

7. You will receive a pop-up menu on your screen. Select the option you prefer.

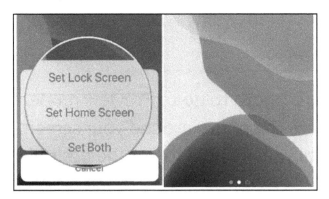

Chapter 17: Screenshots

Screenshots are one way to make a copy of your screen for later use or to share with others.

Take a Screenshot

Here is how to take a screenshot on your iPhone SE.

1. Open the content you want to screenshot.
2. Tap the home button and the power off button at the same time.

3. Your screen will flash immediately, and your screenshot is ready.

Edit and View Screenshots

Your screenshots are automatically saved in the Photos app. Follow the steps below to edit or view your screenshots.

1. Click on **Albums** in the **Photos** app.
2. Tap **Screenshots** to display all the screenshots you took on your phone.
3. Click on a screenshot to view, favorite, share or edit it.
4. To add your screenshots in apps like Messages or Mail, tap the camera icon or the **Edit** menu.

Chapter 18: Safari

Safari is the default web browser for all Apple devices. You can use it to view pages that are open on your other devices, share links, browse the web, and lots more. We will delve more into it in this chapter.

View and Reopen Recently Closed Tabs in Safari

1. Open the **Safari** app.
2. Click on the button at the bottom right side of your screen.
3. Tap and hold the new tab button until you see a list of the Recently Closed Tabs.
4. Click on a site to open the address in a new tab.
5. Tap **Done** to exit.

Recently Closed Tabs	Done
Wikipedia wikipedia.org	

Customize Your Favorite Site in Safari

On the Safari home page, you will find recommended websites, your favorite websites, frequently visited sites and Siri suggestions. This guide will show you how to customize your favorite websites.

1. On the homepage of the Safari browser, under the **Favorites** section, click and hold a website's favicon to display the preview screen as well as the contextual menu. There are a couple other options including **Edit** and **Delete**.

2. Tap **Edit** to rename the site as you
   want it to show on your Favorites.

3. In the website address field, you can
   also enter a different website to take
   you to a different part of that site.

Delete Frequently Visited Sites from the Start Page

The Safari home page always displays your Frequently Visited sites. Follow the steps below to turn this off:

1. Click on **Safari** in the **Settings** app.
2. Turn off the option for **Frequently Visited Sites** in the **General** section.

Save Open Tabs as Bookmark

Save websites of interest as bookmark so that you can go back to the sites at a later time.

1. Type in the web address you wish to visit in the Safari browser.

2. When the site opens, click on  at the bottom of your screen.

3. Then tap **Add Bookmark.**

4. Title your bookmark, then tap the icon under **Location** to select a folder to save the bookmark.

5. Once done, tap **Save.**

Bookmark Multiple Open Tabs in Safari

Follow the steps below to bookmark different websites at once:

1. Open all the sites you plan to bookmark.
2. Let one of the websites be in the main browsing window.
3. Press long on  at the bottom of your screen.

4. Click on **Add Bookmarks for X Tabs** on the next screen.

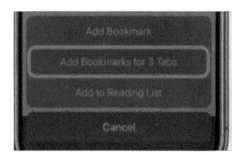

5. On the next screen, save the tabs in a new bookmark folder or choose from current list and click **Save** at the top of the page to save your bookmarks.

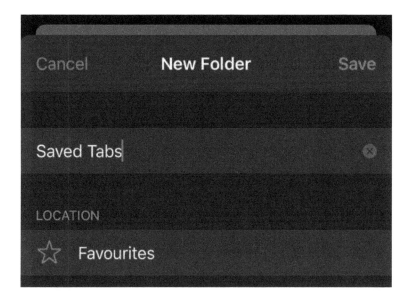

Close All Your Open Tabs at Once

Follow the steps below to close all your open tabs at the same time:

Method 1

1. Open the **Safari** browser.

2. Press long on 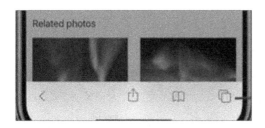 at the right side of the bookmark icon.

3. Select **Close All Tabs.**

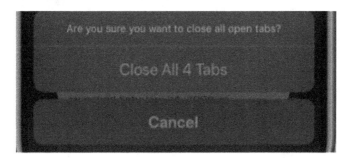

Method 2

1. Tap once on  icon to display the Window view.
2. Press long on **Done.**

3. Select **Close All Tabs.**

Automatically Close Safari Tabs

Set up your browser to close open tabs at defined time.

1. Tap **Safari** in the **Settings** app.
2. Select **Close Tabs.**
3. Select your preferred option on the next screen.

Safari Share Sheet

Follow the steps below to share a web page as a link, archive, or PDF file:

1. Open the website you want to share.

2. Tap  to display the Share Sheet.

3. Click your sharing method from the list. Tap **More** to see other options.

4. Select your sharing method and tap **Options** to choose to send as archive, link or PDF.

Change Where to Store Downloaded Files

All the files you download on Safari are automatically saved in the **Downloads** area within the **Files** app. Follow the steps below to save your downloaded files in a different location:

1. Tap **Safari** in the **Settings** app.
2. Select **Downloads.**
3. Select your preferred download folder on the next screen.

Modify When the Download List Should be Cleared.

By default, Safari clears the download list after 24 hours. However, the steps below will guide you on how to change the setting for clearing the download list.

1. Tap **Safari** in the **Settings** app.
2. Select **Downloads.**
3. Select **Remove Download List Items.**
4. Choose your preferred option on the next screen.

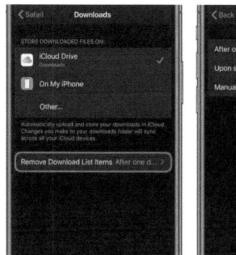

Chapter 19: Family Sharing

Family Sharing permits you to share your purchases with your family members, a maximum of six family members. With family sharing, you can also set up controls and permissions over your children's purchase and content. Every member in a family sharing group will be able to access the purchases of other family members. However, any purchase on the group will be charged to the account of the person that created the group, except if the person making the purchase has enough credit in his/her iTunes account to cover the purchase. Only then will the individual's account be charged. The person that creates the group is known as the family organizer.

Set Up Family Sharing

Follow the steps below to set up family sharing.

1. Click on the Apple ID banner on the top of the **Settings** app home screen.
2. Select **Set Up Family Sharing.**

3. Click **Get Started.**
4. Tap **Add Photo** to set up a photo for the group if desired.
5. Tap **Continue.**
6. Tap **Continue** again on the next screen.

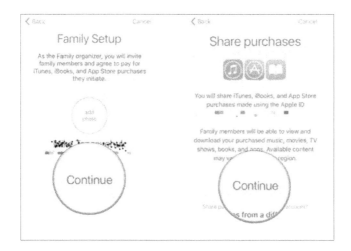

7. Tap **Continue** on the Payment Method screen.

8. Click to share your location with members of the group, or tap **Not Now.**

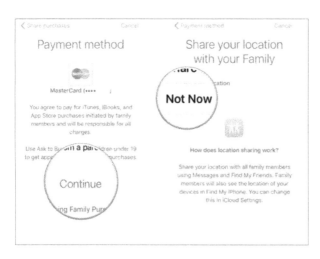

9. Select **Add Family Member.**

10.   Type the name of the family
    members and click on the names to
    add the contacts to the group.
11. Type the security code for your card
    on the next screen as the organizer.

12. You can add up to 6 family members.
    Each contact you add will be notified
    via email along with a push
    notification on their Apple devices to
    either accept or decline joining the
    group.

13. Once the contacts accepts the invite, any purchase they make will be charged to your card.

Accept a Family Sharing Invitation

If someone sends you an invite to join a group, follow the steps below to join the group:

1. Click on the Apple ID banner on the top of the **Settings** app home screen.
2. Tap **Invitations.**

3. Tap the Invitation and click on **Accept** or **Decline** if you do not want to join the group.

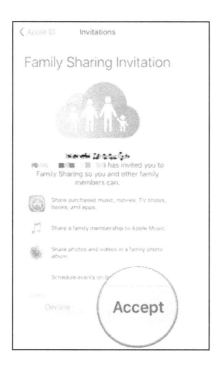

4. Tap **Confirm.**

5. Tap **Continue** within the **Share Purchases** screen.

6. Click to share your location with members of the group, or tap **Not Now.**

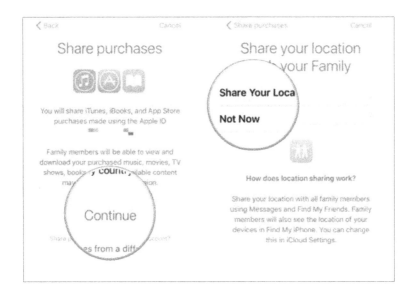

7. Congrats! You are now a member of the group.

Designate Someone as A Parent or Guardian

The Parent can be the second administrator who approves request if the family organizer is not available. Here is how to assign a parent:

1. Click on the Apple ID banner on the top of the **Settings** app home screen.
2. Select **Family Sharing.**

3. Select the contact who you want to act as a parent.

4. Move the switch beside **Parent/ Guardian** to the right to enable it.

Add a Child to Family Sharing

Follow the steps below to add your child to the family sharing group.

1. Click on the Apple ID banner on the top of the **Settings** app home screen.

2. Select **Family Sharing.**
3. Select **Add Family Member.**
4. Then select **Create a Child Account.**

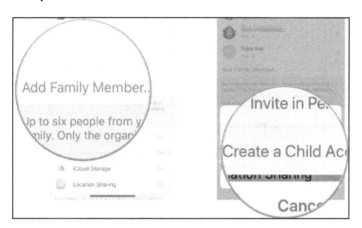

5. Click **Next.**
6. Set the birth date of your child.
7. Tap **Next.**
8. Read through the Parent Privacy Disclosure and tap **Agree.**

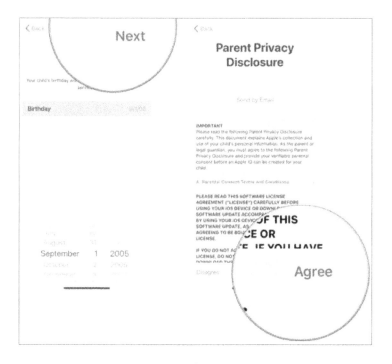

9. Type your card's security code, then tap **Next.**

10.   Type the names of your child and click **Next.**

11. Type an email address to create an Apple account for your child then tap **Next.**

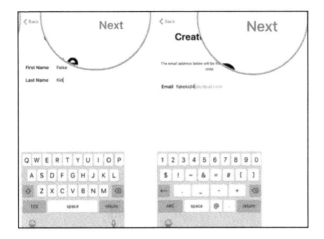

12. Click on **Create.**

13. Set a password, enter the password again.

14.   Tap **Next.**

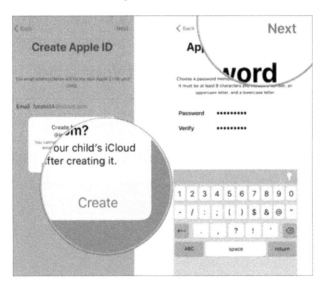

15. Select a security question and type the answer. Repeat until you have set three security questions and answers.

16.   Switch on or off the option for **Ask to Buy,** if you want.

17. Tap **Next.**

18.   Click to share your location with members of the group, or tap **Not Now.**

19.   Read the Terms and Conditions and tap **Agree.**

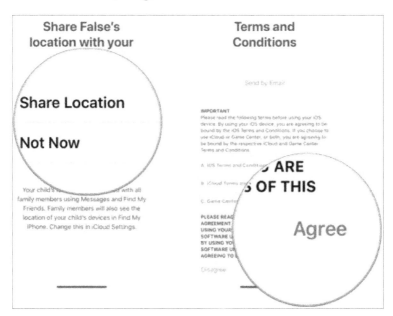

20. Tap **Agree** again.

21. Then read the Terms and Conditions for iTunes and tap **Agree.**

22. Tap **Agree** again to complete setting up your child's account.

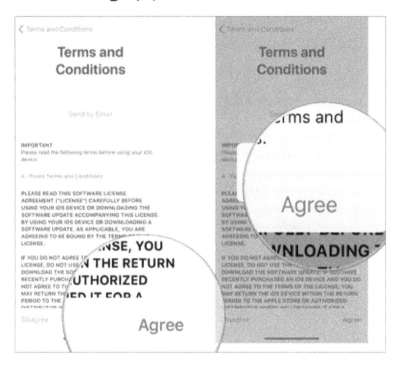

Chapter 20: Dark Mode

Dark mode changes the interface elements and system apps of your device to a deep slate gray or dark color while making the text easy for your eyes to read. This feature is helpful both at night and when you want to preserve battery.

Activate Dark Mode with Control Center

1. Make an upward swipe from the bottom of your screen.
2. Press hard on the Screen Brightness icon.
3. On the next screen, tap **Appearance.**
4. Select either **Light** or **Dark.**

Add Dark Mode Toggle in Control Center

Create a dark mode shortcut in the control center with the steps below:

1. Click on **Control Center** in the home page of the **Settings** app.
2. Select **Customize Controls.**

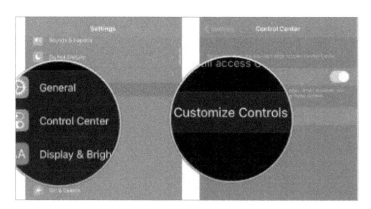

3. Scroll down and click ⊕ beside **Dark Mode.**

4. Click the handles by the right side of the **Dark Mode.** Drag the handle and drop it at the desired location in your control center so that when next you want to switch on Dark mode, you will just go to control center and tap the **Dark Mode** button.

Activate Dark Mode with Settings

1. Tap **Display & Brightness** in the home page of the **Settings** app.

2. On the next screen, tap **Dark** to switch to Dark Mode.

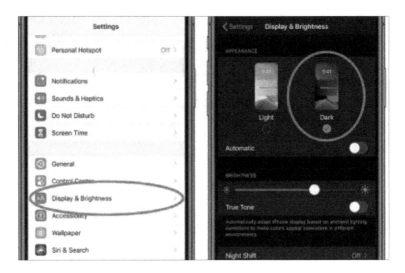

3. If you want your phone to automatically switch between Dark and Light mode, toggle on the option for **Automatic.** With this option enabled, your phone will switch between sunrise and sunset.

4. If you will rather set it up manually, first switch on the **Automatic** button, then click on **Options** under **Automatic.**

5. You will see two options on the next screen. Choose the option that

appeals to you: either **Sunset to Sunrise,** or **Custom Schedule.**

- o Select **Sunset to Sunrise** if you prefer the dark mode to be active between every sunset till the next sunrise.

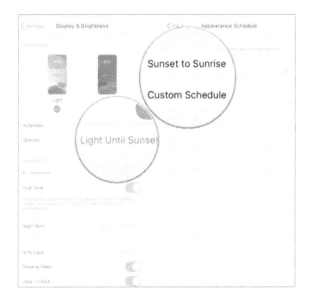

- o Select **Custom Schedule** if you prefer to create your desired time for dark mode to be activated.
- o Tap **Dark Appearance** and choose the times to activate Dark Mode.

- Tap **Light Appearance** and choose the times to activate Light Mode.

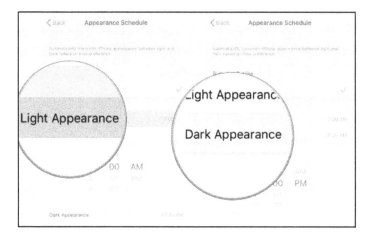

Chapter 21: Animoji and Memoji

The Memoji and Animoji are creative ways to send messages. The iPhone SE have Memoji Sticker packs that can be used by anyone. These stickers also apply to Animojis. Although the Memojis are fixed, there are about twenty-four varieties in the set that allows you to choose the particular emotion you want to display, as well as tons of customization options.

Create a Memoji

While the iPhone SE does not have the feature to create a new Memoji, however, you can customize the Animoji and Memoji on your phone in any way you fit. Follow the steps below to achieve this:

1. Launch the **Messages** app, open an existing conversation or start a new message.

2. Tap the Memoji button on the Message app drawer. If it's not

visible, tap the App store icon to display it.

3. You will find several Memoji options to choose from.
4. Swipe right on the app drawer until you get to the end. Tap the Plus icon to view a blank Memoji canvas.
5. Tap each category like color, skin, hairstyle, etc. and customize the Memoji as you wish.
6. Tap **Done** to save your settings.

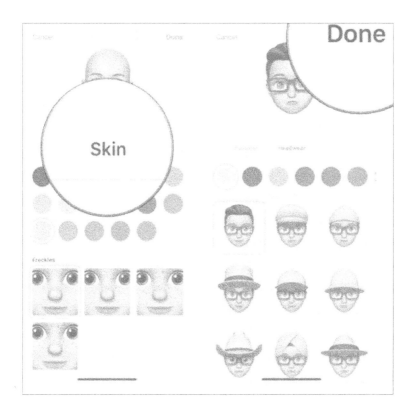

Edit a Memoji

1. Open a new message in the **Messages** app.
2. Tap the Memoji button on the Message app drawer. If it's not visible, tap the App store icon to display it.

3. Scroll through all the available Memoji until you find the one you like, then click on it.
4. Tap the 3-dot icon at the top of your screen.
5. Tap **Edit.**

6. Scroll through the options on the next screen and customize the Memoji as it suits you.

Using Memoji Stickers

1. Launch the messaging app of your choice.
2. Tap  on your keyboard.
3. Scroll through the displayed list and click on any sticker pack you like.

4. Select the desired sticker.

5. Tap  to send.

Share Animoji to Social Networks

1. Launch the **Messages** app.
2. Open the conversation that has the Animoji or Memoji you wish to share.
3. Tap the Animoji.

4. Tap 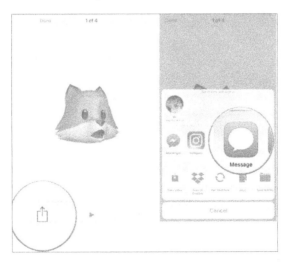 (the share icon)
5. Click on the social network or app that you want to share the Animoji.

6. Then tap 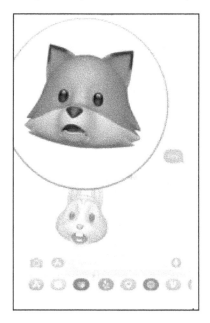 to send.

Save an Animoji to Your Camera Roll

Follow the steps below to save an Animoji in the same way you save videos:

1. Launch the **Messages** app.
2. Open the conversation that has the Animoji or Memoji you wish to save.
3. Tap the Animoji.

4. Tap ⬆️

5. Then tap **Save Video.**

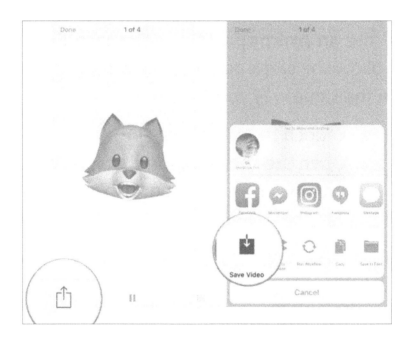

Share Saved Animoji from Camera Roll

Follow the steps above to save an Animoji as a video, then follow the steps below to share the Animoji from your camera roll.

1. Click on **Videos** album in the **Photos** app.

2. Tap the saved Animoji video.

3. Tap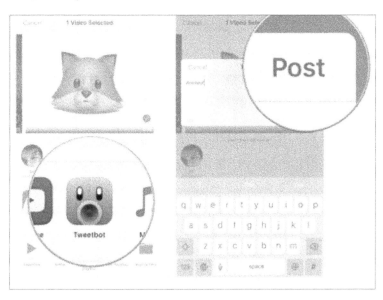

4. Click on the social network or app that you want to share the Animoji.

5. Tap **Post** to share the video.

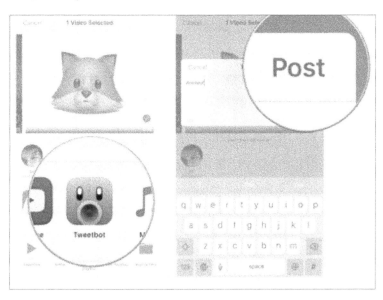

Chapter 22: Messages

The Messages app on the SE allows you to easily share photos and names, send Animoji and Memoji, and so much more. Let's explore the things you can do with the Messages app.

Set a Name and Photo for Your iMessage Profile

Follow the steps below to add your name and picture to your Messaging app.

1. Launch the **Messages** app.

2. Tap ••• at the top right side of your screen.

3. Select **Edit Name and Photo.**

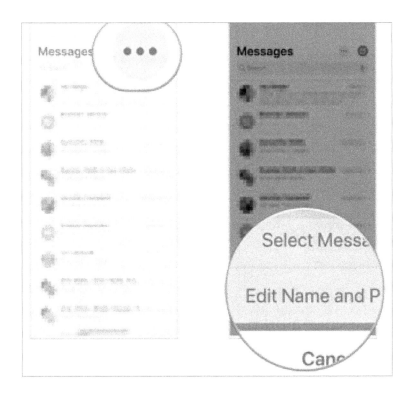

4. Then select **Choose Name and Photo** on the next screen.

5. Input your first and last name, then tap **View More** and choose the photo that you want to use for your profile.

6. Click **Edit** to choose a picture from your album. Alternatively, select an Animoji from the Animojis displayed.

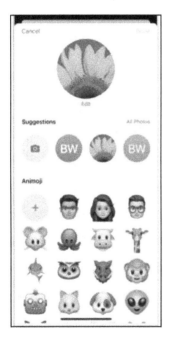

- If you clicked on an Animoji, you will be asked in the next screen to **Select A Pose.** Choose the pose that appeals to you.
- Tap **Next** to get to the **Select a Color** screen.
- Choose the color that you like.

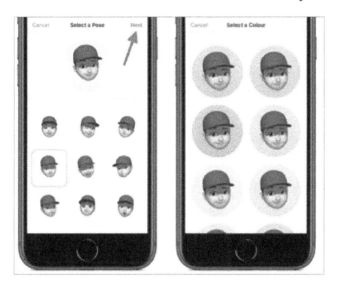

7. Tap **Done** and you will be returned to the Profile name screen.
8. Tap **Continue.**

9. Tap **Use** if you want to use the
   picture for both Apple ID and your
   Contacts. Otherwise, tap **Not Now.**

10.   Tap **Continue.**
11. Select who should be able to view
    your name and picture. Tap **Contacts
    Only** if you want to grant access to
    all your contacts or tap **Always Ask** if
    you want to manually select each
    time you send a message.
12. Tap **Done.**

Change Your Profile Photo

1. Launch the **Messages** app.

2. Tap  at the top right side of your screen.

3. Select **Edit Name and Photo.**

4. Tap **Edit.**

5. Tap **All Photos.**

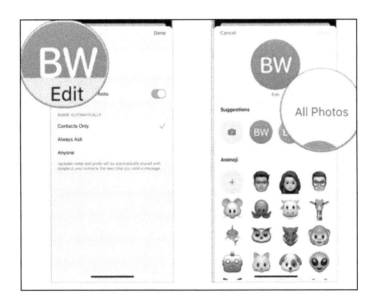

6. Click on the picture you want to use.
7. Fit the picture into the circle.
8. Add your filter.
9. Tap **Done.**

Select Your Initials As Your Profile Picture

Follow the steps below to use your name initials as your profile picture:

1. Launch the **Messages** app.

2. Tap ⋯ at the top right side of your screen.

3. Select **Edit Name and Photo.**

4. Tap **Edit.**
5. In the next screen, under Suggestions, you will find an image that contains your initials. Select the one that you like.
6. Choose your preferred color in the following screen.
7. Tap **Done.**

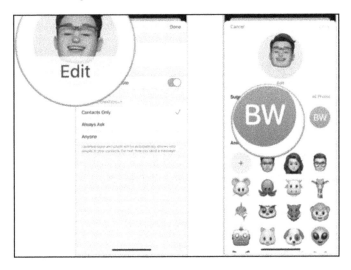

Modify Your Sharing Settings

Follow the steps below to modify who should be able to view your name and picture and who should not:

1. Launch the **Messages** app.

2. Tap ⋯ at the top right side of your screen.

3. Select **Edit Name and Photo.**

4. Go to **Share Name and Photo** and move the button to the right to enable it.

5. Under **Share Automatically,** select your preferred sharing option and tap **Yes** to confirm.

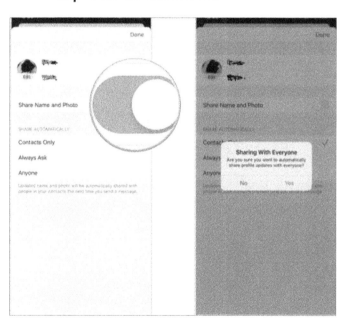

Share Your Profile Name and Photo

Each time you try to send a message or receive a message from an individual who doesn't have the permission to view your profile details, a notification will come into your phone. You can then choose to share the details with the contact. Follow the steps below to share your profile details:

1. Click on the message from the individual.
2. Tap **Share.**

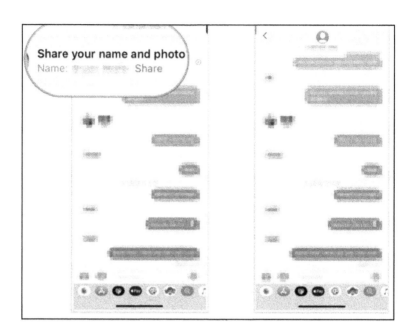

Chapter 23: Turn On Announce Message with Siri

This feature allows Siri to inform you whenever you have an incoming message while putting on your Apple Airpods. Whenever you receive a message, Siri will let you know the name of the sender and also read out the message. However, if the message is long, Siri will only inform you that you have a message as well as the name of the sender. If you want Siri to read out the message, you will need to make a verbal request to Siri.

Below are the headphones that work with this feature:

- 2nd generation Airpods.
- Beats Solo Pro.
- AirPods Pro.
- Powerbeats Pro.

Follow the steps below to set up Message Announcement on your iPhone:

1. Launch the **Settings** app.

2. Tap **Notifications.**
3. Move the switch beside **Announce Messages with Siri** to the right to enable the feature.

How to Reply to Messages

When Siri reads out the message, Siri will go silent waiting for your response. You may choose to have Siri reply the message.

1. The first thing is to let Siri know that you wish to reply the message.
2. Followed by your message. For example, you say something like "Siri Reply" "I will be there".
3. Siri will send the reply once you confirm that the message is okay.

Disable Reply Confirmation

Follow the steps below to have Siri instantly send your response to a message immediately after you are done speaking instead of reading that message back to you.

1. Click on **Notifications** in the **Settings** app.

2. Tap **Announce Messages with Siri.**
3. Switch on the option for **Reply without Confirmation.**

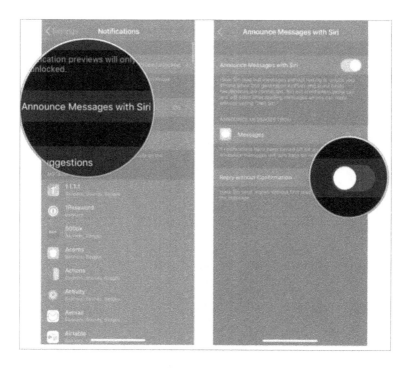

4. To pause Announce Messages with Siri, simply take off your headphones.

Manage 'Announce Messages with Siri'

Follow the steps below to customize Siri to read messages from specified contacts:

1. Click on **Notifications** in the **Settings** app.

2. Tap **Announce Messages with Siri.**

3. Tap **Messages.**
4. Switch on the option for **Announce Messages with Siri.**
5. Underneath **Announce Messages From,** tap the option that suits you.

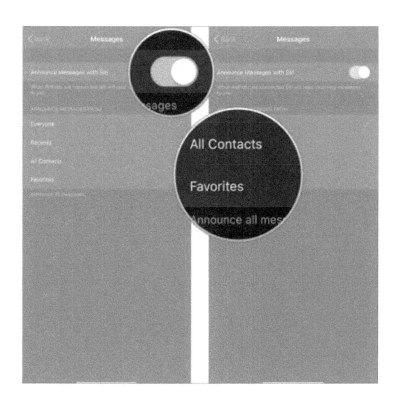

Chapter 24: Gaming

Apple Arcade

Apple Arcade is a gaming subscription service on your iPhone device. It is also available on other Apple devices like the iPad, Apple TV, etc. At a monthly fee of $4.99 or a yearly fee of $49.99, you can download games from several available titles. You can also share all the downloaded games with members of your family sharing group.

Sign Up for Apple Arcade
1. Launch the **App Store.**

2. At the bottom of your screen, tap **Arcade.**

3. You have the first month free. Select **Try It Free** to begin the free trial.
4. Tap **Confirm** to begin your subscription.

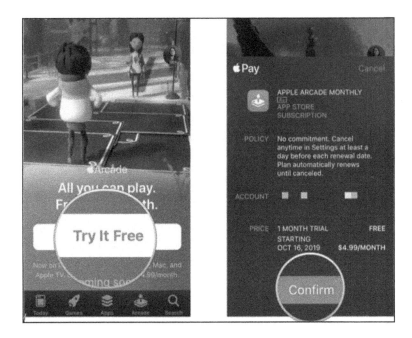

Cancel Apple Arcade

Follow the steps below to unsubscribe from Apple Arcade:

1. Launch the **App Store.**
2. Select your Apple ID at the top.
3. Tap **Subscriptions.**

4. Tap **Apple Arcade.**

5. To stop the free trial, tap **Cancel Free Trial,** or tap **Cancel Subscription** to cancel charged subscription.

6. Confirm your action.

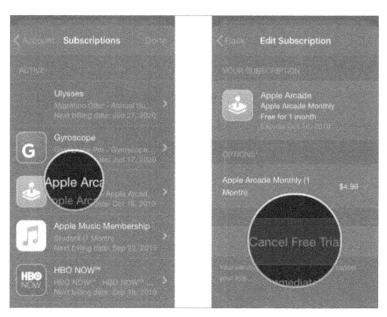

Use Family Sharing with Apple Arcade

To share downloaded games with members of your Family sharing group, launch the App store and go to the **Arcade tab.**

Select and Start Playing Game

Here is your guide on choosing and playing a game:

1. Launch the **App Store**.
2. At the bottom of your screen, tap **Arcade.**

3. Scroll through the available games and click on the one that you want.
4. Then tap **Get** to begin download.

5. Once the download is complete, tap **Play** to enjoy your new game.
6. You can also find a shortcut in your home screen.

Play On a Different Device

You can save your downloaded games in iCloud so that whenever you are logged into the same Apple ID on a different device, you can re-download the game and play from where you stopped.

The steps below will guide you to manage your games in the iCloud storage:

1. Tap your Apple ID at the top of the **Settings** app.
2. Select **iCloud.**
3. Tap **Manage Storage.**

4. Scroll to the game or app you are interested in and click on it.

5. If you want to remove the game data from iCloud, tap **Delete Document and Data**.

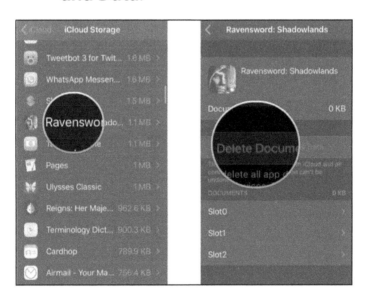

Troubleshooting Apple Arcade

The tips below will help to solve any issues you may have with the Apple Arcade:

1. Ensure that Family Sharing is correctly set up.
2. If you are experiencing issues downloading games, sign out of your Apple ID then sign in using the same details.
3. If the above doesn't work, you may reboot or reset your device.

Pair Your DualShock 4 Controller

Pair your controller with your phone to have a great gaming experience.

1. Click on **Bluetooth** in the **Settings** app.
2. Press the **PlayStation** and the **SHARE** button on the controller until a white light begins to flash. This is done to have it in pairing mode.

3. The controller will be listed in the Bluetooth menu, underneath the **Other Devices** section. Tap the controller to pair it with your iPhone SE.

Pair Your Phone with Your Xbox One S Controller

1. Click on **Bluetooth** in the **Settings** app.
2. Switch on your Xbox. Then press down the button on the top of the

controller for approximately 3 seconds, to have it in pairing mode.

3. The controller will be listed in the Bluetooth menu, underneath the **Other Devices** section as **Xbox One S Controller**. Tap the controller to pair it with your iPhone SE.

Unpair your Xbox One S Controller or DualShock 4 Controller

Here is how to disconnect the controller from your phone:

1. Click on **Bluetooth** in the **Settings** app.
2. You will find the controller among the list on your screen. Tap
3. Tap **Forget This Device.**
4. Then click **OK.**

Chapter 25: Clear Storage Space on iPhone SE

If you ever run out of storage space on your new device, the steps below will help you to free up the needed space.

Review and Delete Personal Videos

One quick way to make space on your phone is to go through the videos you shot on your iPhone and delete the ones that you no longer need.

1. Tap **General** in the **Settings** app.
2. Select **iPhone Storage.**
3. Select **Show All.**

4. Select **Review Personal Videos.**
5. Select the video you plan to delete.
6. Tap
7. Then click **Delete From This iPhone.**

Review Large Attachments on iPhone

Images, gifs, and other media that you send or receive via the Messaging apps turn to attachments that take up your storage space. You can review these attachments with the steps below:

1. Tap **General** in the **Settings** app.
2. Select **iPhone Storage.**

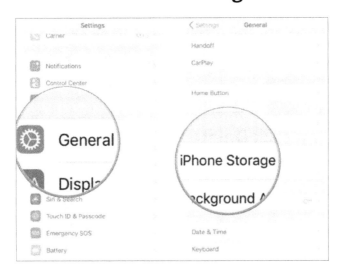

3. Select **Messages**. This is close to the bottom of your screen.
4. Click on **Review Large Attachments.**

5. Now you can review any attachment received in the messaging app. You can also delete the attachments.

Offload Unused Apps

We all have that app that we haven't used in a long time eating up space. Your new iPhone SE can help to offload apps that you have not used for a certain period, while retaining the data for that app. The app icon for the deleted app will stay on your home screen for easy re-installation. Follow the steps below to enable **Offload Unused Apps.**

1. Select **iTunes & App Store** in the **Settings** app.
2. Move the switch beside **Offload Unused Apps** to the right to enable the feature.
3. Once activated, your device will automatically delete any apps you do not use after some time.

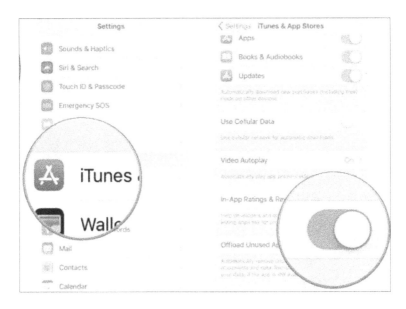

Disable 'Offload Unused Data'

1. Select **iTunes & App Store** in the **Settings** app.

2. Move the switch beside **Offload Unused Apps** to the left to disable the feature.

Manually Offload App

This method allows you to manually offload your unused apps.

1. Tap **General** in the **Settings** app.
2. Click on **iPhone Storage.**
3. Select the app you want to offload.
4. Click on **Offload App.**
5. Select **Offload App** from the popup menu on your screen.

Re-install Offloaded Apps

Offloaded apps are not totally deleted from your phone as the app icon remains on your home screen. If you find that you need an offloaded app back, you can follow any of the two methods below to restore offloaded apps.

Method 1

1. Tap **General** in the Settings app.
2. Click on **iPhone Storage.**
3. Select the offloaded app.
4. Select **Reinstall App.**

Method 2

1. Tap the icon for the offloaded app in your home screen to install the app again.

Restrict App Offload

Follow the steps below to stop others from enabling the **App Offload** feature:

1. Launch the **Settings** app.
2. Tap **Screen Time.**
3. Move the switch beside **Content & Privacy Restrictions** to the right to enable it.
4. Select **iTunes & App Store Purchases** in the same screen.
5. Click **Deleting App.**
6. Then select **Don't Allow.**

Chapter 26: Conclusion

This book has extensively touched on all the important features of the operating system for iPhones. The aim of writing this book is to ensure that you do not miss any detail that would help you to be productive when utilizing your phone.

If you are pleased with the content of this book, don't forget to recommend this book to a friend.

Thank you.

www.ingramcontent.com/pod-product-compliance
Lightning Source LLC
LaVergne TN
LVHW041208050326
832903LV00021B/524